W9-BML-772

# How to Use This Book

**Look for these special features in this book:**

**SIDEBARS**, **CHARTS**, **GRAPHS**, and original **MAPS** expand your understanding of what's being discussed—and also make useful sources for class-room reports.

**FAQs** answer common **F**requently **A**sked **Q**uestions about people, places, and things.

**WOW FACTORS** offer "Who knew?" facts to keep you thinking.

**TRAVEL GUIDE** gives you tips on exploring the state—either in person or right from your chair!

**PROJECT ROOM** provides fun ideas for school assignments and incredible research projects. Plus, there's a guide to primary sources—what they are and how to cite them.

Please note: All statistics are as up-to-date as possible at the time of publication.
Population data is taken from the 2010 census.

Consultants: Geoffrey Cook, Department of Geosciences, University of Rhode Island;
Evelyn Sterne, Department of History, University of Rhode Island; William Loren Katz;
Catherine DeCesare, History Coordinator, University of Rhode Island

Book production by The Design Lab

Library of Congress Cataloging-in-Publication Data
Burgan, Michael.
 Rhode Island / by Michael Burgan. — Revised edition.
    pages cm. — (America the beautiful. Third series)
 Includes bibliographical references and index.
 ISBN 978-0-531-28291-5 (library binding : alk. paper)
 1. Rhode Island—Juvenile literature. I. Title.
 F79.3.B87 2014
 974.5—dc23                                    2013044802

©2015, 2009 Scholastic Inc.
All rights reserved. Published in 2015 by Children's Press, an imprint of Scholastic Inc.
Printed in the United States of America 141
SCHOLASTIC, CHILDREN'S PRESS, and associated logos are trademarks and/or
registered trademarks of Scholastic Inc.

1 2 3 4 5 6 7 8 9 10 R 24 23 22 21 20 19 18 17 16 15

America ★ the ★ beautiful

Revised Edition

# Rhode Island

BY MICHAEL BURGAN

Third Series, Revised Edition

Children's Press®
An Imprint of Scholastic Inc.
New York ★ Toronto ★ London ★ Auckland ★ Sydney
Mexico City ★ New Delhi ★ Hong Kong
Danbury, Connecticut

# CONTENTS

# GROWTH AND CHANGE

## 4

Rhode Island is the birthplace of the American Industrial Revolution. Workers and immigrants struggle to gain their political rights. . . . . . . **48**

# MORE MODERN TIMES

## 5

Rhode Islanders survive the Great Depression and eagerly do their part in World War II. After the war, workers move to the suburbs, factories move out of state, and new industries move in. . . **62**

Explore Rhode Island's spectacular shoreline, rich history, and fun-filled towns. . . . . **104**

## 9

# TRAVEL GUIDE

MASSACHUSETTS

Blackstone
River Rapids

Slater Mill

WOONSOCKET

Seagrave Memorial
Observatory

Chepachet

Blackstone

Jerimoth
Hill

Rhode Island School
of Design Museum

PROVIDENCE

PAWTUCKET

Crescent Park
Carousel

SCITUATE

Roger
Williams
Park Zoo

MASSACHUSETTS

Conimicut
Point Park

Pawtuxet

Coggeshall Farm Museum

New England Wireless
and Steam Museum

Providence

BRISTOL

Herreshoff
Marine
Museum

WARWICK

RHODE
ISLAND

Narragansett Bay

Butterfly
Zoo

Sakonnet

Rhode
Island

CONNECTICUT

Quonset Air
Museum

Wood

NEWPORT

Rhode Island Sound

Pawcatuck

CHARLESTOWN

Rose Island
Lighthouse

New England Aquarium
Exploration Center

WESTERLY

Block Island Sound

Block
Island

ATLANTIC
OCEAN

**QUICK FACTS**

**State capital:** Providence
**Largest city:** Providence
**Total area:** 1,545 square miles
(4,002 sq km)
**Highest point:** Jerimoth Hill,
812 feet (247 m) above sea level
**Lowest point:** Sea level along
the Atlantic Ocean

0          10
Miles

# Welcome to Rhode Island!

## HOW DID RHODE ISLAND GET ITS NAME?

In 1524, Italian explorer Giovanni da Verrazzano spotted a triangle-shaped island in the Atlantic Ocean, about 10 miles (16 kilometers) from the mainland. He thought the small spot of land looked like Rhodes, an island that is part of Greece. Just over a century later, English colonists came to the region Verrazzano had explored. They called their new home Rhode Island, thinking it was the island Verrazzano had seen. Their settlement and others near the town of Providence soon merged to form a colony. When the colony became a state, its official name changed to the State of Rhode Island and Providence Plantations—a long name for the smallest state in the nation!

RHODE ISLAND

# READ ABOUT

A view of the
Atlantic Ocean
from Block Island

# CHAPTER ONE

# LAND

★

ONE OF RHODE ISLAND'S NICK-
NAMES IS THE OCEAN STATE, AND
WITH GOOD REASON. From Rhode
Island's highest point on Jerimoth Hill, 812 feet
(247 meters), to its lowest point at sea level, the
Atlantic Ocean is never more than a half-hour
drive away.

Rhode Island covers just 1,545 square miles
(4,002 square kilometers), making it the smallest of the 50 U.S. states. This explains another
of its nicknames—Little Rhody.

## WORD TO KNOW

**glaciers** *slow-moving masses of ice*

## CARVING THE LAND

The movement of huge sheets of ice called **glaciers** helped form Rhode Island's rivers and rocky shores. Ice several thousand feet thick covered the region that is now Rhode Island at least two different times. The moving ice ground down hills and carved out the river valleys and coastline. As the ice melted, some of the water was trapped in low spots, forming lakes. The last glacier left Rhode Island about 15,000 years ago.

## LAND REGIONS

Rhode Island is one of the six states that form New England. It borders two states: Connecticut to the west and Massachusetts to the north and east. The southern part of Rhode Island lies along the Atlantic Ocean.

# Rhode Island Geo-Facts

Along with the state's geographical highlights, this chart ranks Rhode Island's land, water, and total area compared to all other states.

**Total area; rank** . . . . . . . . 1,545 square miles (4,002 sq km); 50th
**Land; rank** . . . . . . . . . 1,045 square miles (2,707 sq km); 50th
**Water; rank** . . . . . . . . . .500 square miles (1,295 sq km); 41st
**Inland water; rank** . . . . . .178 square miles (461 sq km); 46th
**Coastal water; rank** . . . . . . . .9 square miles (23 sq km); 20th
**Territorial water; rank** . . .314 square miles (813 sq km); 17th
**Geographic center** . . . Kent, 1 mile (1.6 km) southwest of Crompton
**Latitude** . . . . . . . . . . . . . . . . . . . . . . . . 41°09' N to 42°01' N
**Longitude** . . . . . . . . . . . . . . . . . . . . . . 71°07' W to 71°53' W
**Highest point** . . . . . . Jerimoth Hill, 812 feet (247 m) above sea level
**Lowest point** . . . . . . . . . . . . . . Sea level along the Atlantic Ocean
**Largest city** . . . . . . . . . . . . . . . . . . . . . . . . . . . . . . Providence
**Longest river** . . . . . . . . . . . . . . . . . . . . . . . . . . . . . Blackstone

Source: U.S. Census Bureau; U.S. Geological Survey, 2010 census

 **Rhode Island could fit into Alaska, the largest state, 429 times!**

# Rhode Island Topography

Use the color-coded elevation chart to see on the map Rhode Island's high points (orange) and low points (green to dark green). Elevation is measured as the distance above or below sea level.

| Elevation | | |
|---|---|---|
| Feet | | Meters |
| 800 | — | 244 |
| 600 | — | 183 |
| 400 | — | 122 |
| 200 | — | 61 |

MASSACHUSETTS

Woonsocket

Blackstone

Chepachet

Valley Falls
Pawtucket

Jerimoth Hill

Scituate

Providence

EASTERN

Cranston

MASSACHUSETTS

East Providence

Foster NEW

Scituate Reservoir

Pawtuxet

Barrington    Warren

ENGLAND

West Warwick

UPLAND

Warwick

Bristol

Greene

COASTAL LOWLANDS

East Greenwich

Prudence Island

Tiverton

CONNECTICUT

Portsmouth

Narragansett Bay

Sakonnet

Wickford

Rhode Island

Wood

Pawcatuck

Newport

Conanicut Island

Charlestown

Rhode Island Sound

Westerly

Point Judith

Block Island Sound

ATLANTIC OCEAN

BLOCK ISLAND

New Shoreham

| 0 | | 10 Miles |
| 0 | | 10 Kilometers |

Rhode Island is divided into two major land regions. The western half of the state is the Eastern New England Upland. The rest of the state, including the islands that dot Narragansett Bay and the Atlantic Ocean, are part of the Coastal Lowlands.

**Boys fishing along the Blackstone River**

## The Eastern New England Upland

The New England Upland stretches across the northeastern United States and into Canada, and part of its eastern region is located in Rhode Island. This area features forests, rocky hills, and small mountains, along with fertile river valleys that are good for farming. The Blackstone River, which flows from the highlands down into Narragansett Bay, was used to power many of the state's early mills.

In Rhode Island, the elevation of the upland increases from the center of the state to its northwest corner. The town of Foster near the Connecticut border is the site of Jerimoth Hill.

## The Coastal Lowlands

The flat Coastal Lowlands region, which borders the Atlantic Ocean, covers much of Rhode Island. Narragansett Bay, a branch of the Atlantic, slices deeply into the eastern part of the state. The bay is 28 miles (45 km) long, and its many inlets and islands contribute to Rhode Island's more than 400 miles (650 km) of coastline. Rocks and cliffs cover much of the bay's shoreline, though the coast along the Atlantic has sandy beaches.

Narragansett Bay has many islands. The city of Newport is on Aquidneck, the largest of these islands. Next to it is Conanicut Island, which is also called Jamestown. Block Island is the state's one main island in the Atlantic. Ferries run to Block Island, a popular vacation spot.

## CLIMATE

Summers in Rhode Island tend to be hot and wet. Providence, the state's capital and largest city, has an average high temperature of 83 degrees Fahrenheit (28 degrees Celsius) in July. When summer heat builds, thunderstorms sometimes blow in from the west, bring-

### SEE IT HERE!

#### MOHEGAN BLUFFS

One of the most striking natural wonders on Block Island is Mohegan Bluffs, cliffs that tower 200 feet (60 m) above the ocean. Glaciers carved the cliffs many thousands of years ago. Since then, the pounding waters of the Atlantic have been eroding, or wearing away, the cliffs. A sandy beach at the base of the bluffs offers a spectacular view.

# Weather Report

**TEMPERATURE 104°F**  **TEMPERATURE –28°F**

This chart shows record temperatures (high and low) for the state, as well as average temperatures (July and January) and average annual precipitation.

**Record high temperature** . . . . . . . . . . . . . . . . . . 104°F (40°C) at Providence on August 2, 1975

**Record low temperature** . . . . . . . . –28°F (–33°C) at Wood River Junction on January 11, 1942

**Average July temperature, Providence** . . . . . . . . .74°F (23°C)

**Average January temperature, Providence** . . . . . . 29°F (–2°C)

**Average yearly precipitation, Providence** . .47 inches (119 cm)

Source: National Climatic Data Center, NESDIS, NOAA, U.S. Dept. of Commerce

# THE HURRICANE OF 1938

The trouble started with the rain—days of it. Then the massive storm came ashore. On September 21, 1938, a hurricane packing wind gusts of 175 miles per hour (282 kph) plowed straight into Rhode Island. Along the Atlantic Coast, a wave of water 30 feet (9 m) high crashed into Westerly and nearby towns, killing about 100 people and destroying every building in its path. The wave, called a storm surge, then continued northward into Providence. That surge and overflowing rivers flooded the capital city and other towns in the state. The water tossed boats and cars thousands of feet and even took down brick walls. In the days that followed, thousands of volunteers came to Rhode Island to help residents repair the damage.

Rhode Island is sometimes hit by destructive nor'easters.

## Q: WHAT IS A NOR'EASTER?

A: A nor'easter is a powerful storm that forms in the Atlantic Ocean and moves up the East Coast of the United States. Most nor'easters occur during the winter months, and the storms typically dump large amounts of rain or snow. The word *nor'easter* is a shortened form of *northeaster*, and it refers to winds that blow out of the northeast during the storm.

ing cooler air. In the winter, snowstorms are frequent. An average of 35 inches (89 centimeters) of snow falls on the state every year.

Large storms called nor'easters sometimes roar up the Atlantic Coast and slam into Rhode Island. They might bring more than 1 foot (30 cm) of snow. Intense rains can also cause problems. In March 2010, record rainfall in the state caused rivers and streams to burst from their banks. Homes, shopping malls, and train tracks were flooded.

 In August 2011, Hurricane Irene slammed into Rhode Island, uprooting trees and leaving nearly 500,000 homes and businesses without power.

# Rhode Island's National Park Areas

This map shows some of Rhode Island's national parks, monuments, preserves, and other areas protected by the National Park Service.

| | |
|---|---|
| | National Park area |
| NHC | National Heritage Corridor |
| NHS | National Historic Site |
| NMEM | National Memorial |

MASSACHUSETTS

Blackstone

Chepachet

Woonsocket

John H. Chafee Blackstone River Valley NHC

Chepachet

Valley Falls

Pawtucket

Roger Williams NMEM

Scituate

Providence

MASSACHUSETTS

Cranston

East Providence

Pawtuxet

Providence

CONNECTICUT

Warwick

Bristol

Tiverton

Portsmouth

Narragansett Bay

Wood

Wickford

Rhode Island

Sakonnet

N W E S

Pawcatuck

Newport

Touro Synagogue NHS

Rhode Island Sound

Charlestown

Westerly

Block Island Sound

ATLANTIC OCEAN

Block Island

| 0 | 10 Miles |
|---|---|
| 0 | 10 Kilometers |

White trillium

## PLANT LIFE

The state's upland forests are filled with hardwood trees, including oak, cedar, walnut, and red maple, the state tree. In the fall, the leaves of these trees turn brilliant reds, oranges, and yellows. Wildflowers such as violets, trilliums, and irises also brighten the landscape.

The shore is home to saltmeadow grass, cordgrass, saltwort, and other plants that thrive in wet areas. Marsh lavender has tiny purple flowers that stand out among the green and brown surroundings.

## ANIMAL LIFE

Hundreds of different kinds of animals populate Rhode Island. Black bears, deer, and rabbits live in the forest. Otters frolic in Rhode Island's streams, while harbor seals lounge on rocks along the coast. Giant finback, humpback, and right whales swim in the waters near Rhode Island. Sea turtles also make trips to Rhode Island's ocean waters, while smaller turtles make their homes along streams.

Harbor seals rest on Block Island.

A great black-billed gull captures a spider crab at Sachuest Point National Wildlife Refuge, located in Middletown.

## WILDLIFE IN DANGER

The U.S. government keeps a list of all wildlife that is in danger of dying out. Rhode Island has only a few animals on that list, but dozens of others could become **endangered** in the future. Rhode Island's endangered species include the leatherback and hawksbill, two sea turtles, and a bug called the American burying beetle. This busy bug buries dead bodies of animals and birds to store them for food. State officials are also concerned about the bobcat and several kinds of waterfowl.

Considering the state is nick-named the Ocean State, you'd expect to find plenty of fish and shellfish in Rhode Island's waters, and you do! Common fish include flounder, sturgeon, and eel. Lobsters as well as clams called quahogs often turn up on dinner tables across the state.

Hundreds of different types of birds live in or pass through Rhode Island. Robins and blue jays are common in cities and forests, while laughing loons and majestic egrets stick close to the state's waters. Game birds include partridges and wild turkeys.

**Leatherback turtle**

## WORD TO KNOW

**endangered** *in danger of becoming extinct*

Volunteers for Save the Bay work to preserve eelgrass, an aquatic plant that is nearly extinct in Rhode Island waters.

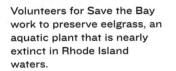

## WORD TO KNOW

**reservoir** *an artificial lake or tank for storing water*

# Water, Water, Everywhere?

Could a state surrounded by water not have enough to drink? That's the question on some Rhode Islanders' minds. The growth of suburbs and industry in the southern part of the state has led some people to call for drilling wells in the Big River Management Area. The area is home to forests, wetlands, and several rivers, including the Big, Nooseneck, Congdon, and Carr. Homeowners need water to drink, cook, and clean, and some businesses go through huge amounts of water every day. In 2010, Amy Kempe, a spokesperson for then governor Donald Carcieri, said, "It's very simple—provide residents quality drinking water and also recognize that this is an economic development tool." Some Rhode Islanders, though, say the solution is not so easy. Building the wells and piping that would bring the water to the necessary places would be expensive. Opponents also have other concerns, such as who would receive the water and who would pay for building the system. Bill Falcone, former Rhode Island Water Resources Board chief of staff, has proposed a different solution. "If you want economic development, build a **reservoir**, because we're going to need [more] water eventually."

THINK ABOUT IT!

## HUMANS AND THE ENVIRONMENT

Wherever people live, they affect the land and water around them. The population of southern Rhode Island has increased dramatically in recent years. The construction of housing developments and office parks can destroy wetlands, and it increases the demand for water.

Human activity poses dangers to Narragansett Bay and the wildlife that relies on it. When humans build near the water, they destroy the homes and food supplies of animals. Pollution from cities and farms also fouls the bay's water.

Since 1970, an organization called Save the Bay has worked to improve the health of Narragansett Bay. Its members have planted marsh grasses that make appealing homes for many kinds of fish. Save the Bay has also stopped the construction of large power plants near the bay. The plants would have produced harmful pollution.

The state's Department of Environmental Management also plays a part in protecting Rhode Island's most precious natural resource. It enforces laws that both limit pollution and protect wildlife in and around the bay.

**MINI-BIO**

### JACK REED: PROTECTING THE ENVIRONMENT

U.S. senator Jack Reed (1949–) of Rhode Island is leading the fight to clean up and preserve Rhode Island's resources and natural beauty. Reed has helped Rhode Island receive millions of dollars from the federal government to safeguard the state's fish and wildlife populations and to protect open lands. Speaking about his state's water concerns, Reed said, "Upgrading our [America's] water infrastructure is essential to ensuring quality water service for Rhode Islanders." As chairman of the Senate Appropriations Subcommittee on Interior, Environment, and Related Agencies, he works closely with government agencies to create laws that benefit the environment.

**?** **Want to know more?** Visit www.factsfornow .scholastic.com and enter the keywords **Rhode Island**.

# READ ABOUT

Early people in the region learned to hunt with bows and arrows.

## c. 12,000 BCE
*The last ice age ends in Rhode Island*

## c. 8000 BCE
*The first humans come to Rhode Island*

Quahog clams

## ▲ c. 2500 BCE
*People live in Greenwich Cove on Narragansett Bay*

# CHAPTER TWO

# FIRST PEOPLE

★

FOURTEEN THOUSAND YEARS AGO, THE GLACIERS WERE LEAVING THE AREA THAT WOULD BECOME RHODE ISLAND. At the time, no humans lived in the region. But as the weather slowly warmed, people began arriving in the area. Rhode Island became home to hunters, fishers, gatherers, and later, farmers who relied on the bounty of the land and sea.

**c. 1200 CE**
*Algonquians
begin to raise
corn*

**1500**
*Narragansetts are
the dominant people
in Rhode Island*

**c. 500 BCE**
*The region's first known
year-round village is
established on Block Island*

Archaeologists have found arrowheads and other Native artifacts in Rhode Island.

## WORDS TO KNOW

**archaeologists** *people who study the remains of past human societies*

**artifacts** *items created by humans, usually for a practical purpose*

**When the English came to Rhode Island, they traded with the Native Americans for wampum and sometimes used it as money.**

## THE FIRST RHODE ISLANDERS

The earliest signs of human life in the region date back about 10,000 years. Hunters and fishers came into southern New England during warmer months seeking food. Near Greenwich Cove on Narragansett Bay, **archaeologists** have found **artifacts** about 4,500 years old. These include stone arrowheads and pieces of pottery.

The first known year-round village in Rhode Island, and perhaps all of New England, was on Block Island. It dates from about 500 BCE. The indigenous, or native, people who lived in this village ate shellfish, seals, and birds. They also gathered wild berries and nuts.

## EARLY WAYS OF LIFE

Most of the early people of Rhode Island settled along rivers or the coast. For the groups along Narragansett Bay and the ocean, the quahog clam was an important source of food. Its shell also had great value. Using stone tools, skilled craftsmen drilled beads from purple spots on the shells. These beads, along with white ones made from whelk shells, were called wampum. They were strung together to create belts. The pattern of the beads could

# Native American Peoples

## (Before European Contact)

This map shows the general area of Native American peoples before European settlers arrived.

## SEE IT HERE!

### STONES FROM THE PAST

Early Native Americans in Rhode Island used stone to create long-lasting tools. You can see stone tools that are thousands of years old at the Tomaquag Indian Memorial Museum of Exeter. The museum has a collection of stone arrowheads, spear points, scrapers, and other tools. Tomaquag also features exhibits that describe the life of modern-day Narragansetts from Rhode Island.

be used to record historical events. Wampum was often exchanged to show good relations between families or groups, and some people were buried with it.

## ALGONQUIANS

The Native people of North America spoke many different languages. Algonquian was the major language of groups in what is now the northeastern United States. Various groups in Rhode Island spoke related versions of this language. The people who spoke the Algonquian language are called Algonquian people.

By 1600 CE, Narragansetts, who lived west of the bay eventually named for them, were the largest Native group in Rhode Island. There were about 20,000 of them. The Wampanoag people lived east of the bay and on some of its islands. Their lands extended into what is now Massachusetts. Rhode Island was also home to smaller groups including Niantics, Pawtuxets, and Cowesetts. The Manissean people lived on Block Island.

Native corn

## EVERYDAY LIFE

Most Algonquians set up camp in one location for the warmer months, when they hunted, fished, and gathered food. They built small, dome-shaped homes called wigwams, which had stick frames covered with animal skins, tree bark, or mats made from plants. A hole in the top of the wigwam let out the smoke from a fire that kept everyone warm. Most people moved to other camps as the weather turned cold. At these camps, they often built structures called longhouses, which could hold up to 20 families.

Algonquians used boats for fishing and transportation. To build canoes, they cut down trees and used fire to hollow them out. They also made a much lighter type of canoe by covering a wooden frame with birch bark.

Algonquians built wigwams from animal skins, sticks, tree bark, and other plant materials.

Around 1200 CE, Algonquians learned about corn, a crop they could grow for food. Native people in Mexico had first raised corn several thousand years earlier. Slowly, corn seeds and the knowledge about how to raise corn spread across North America. Soon Algonquians were growing beans and squash as well, and the three crops were sometimes called the "three sisters."

For the Algonquian people of Rhode Island, daily activities often focused on food—finding it, raising it, or preparing it for meals. Men hunted and fished. Sometimes they used nets to trap the fish. They also caught fish using baited hooks.

## FAQ

**Q: WHY WERE CORN, BEANS, AND SQUASH CALLED THE "THREE SISTERS"?**

**A:** The term reflects the close relationship among those crops in an Algonquian field. Algonquians planted corn and bean seeds together in a small mound. The bean plants added nitrogen to the soil. This chemical helped the corn grow. As it grew, the corn supported the vines of the bean plant. The squash was planted in between the mounds. It grew along the ground, helping to stop the growth of weeds.

Narragansett women had special helpers with their farmwork—tamed hawks! These fast flyers scared away other birds that tried to steal corn or other crops.

Algonquians had many different methods of hunting. They used bows and arrows to shoot deer, geese, and ducks. They set traps to catch foxes and beavers.

When not searching for food, the men made tools out of stone and wood. They also competed in races and shooting contests, played lacrosse and a game similar to soccer, and enjoyed *puim*, which was similar to a card game that used short reeds instead of cards.

Algonquian women raised crops and walked along the shore gathering shellfish. The women smoked and dried the fish that the men caught, preserving it for future meals. Women also built and took down wigwams. Other duties included making mats and clay pots, turning deerskin into leather clothing, and raising children.

Children helped their mothers tend the crops and gather nuts, berries, firewood, and shellfish. As boys grew older, their fathers taught them to hunt. Algonquian children didn't go to school. By watching and listening to the adults around them, they learned about their culture and the proper way to act.

## A WORLD OF SPIRITS

The Algonquian people of Rhode Island believed that a sacred force, called *manitou*, filled everything in the universe. They traced both good and bad events—from powerful storms to successful hunts—to this unseen power. Spirits watching over humans also had manitou in them. Algonquians called on these spirits to help during difficult times.

According to Algonquian belief, the water manitou was a giant horned serpent. In the sky, manitou took the form of a creature called the thunderbird. Other beings were thought to have given Algonquians corn and created the rest of the universe.

To contact manitou and the spirit world, Algonquians relied on people called *powwaws*, also known as shamans. Powwaws were thought to learn the future through their dreams. They used medicines made from plants to cure the sick. They also called on the spirits to help cure people. Sometimes, the powwaws smoked tobacco, which was said to help them contact the spirit world. Algonquians also smoked tobacco during important meetings and ceremonies. Among the Algonquian people, tobacco was the only crop raised by men.

Any male Algonquian, not just a powwaw, could seek help from the spirits during a vision quest. In a vision quest, a teenager went out into the woods alone. He neither ate nor drank as he waited for a vision that would guide him in what he should do with his life.

## STORYTELLER AND TEACHER

When children today want to know about Rhode Island's distant past, they often gather around Paulla "Sunflower" Dove Jennings (1939–). Jennings, who belongs to the Narragansett Nation, is a storyteller who vividly recounts the history of her people. She is the author of the book *Strawberry Thanksgiving*, which explains Narragansett beliefs about how the first strawberries appeared. She has also been a teacher and a member of the Narragansett council.

Native American powwaw

## A NEW ERA

In 1500, the Algonquians of Rhode Island were living a mostly peaceful life. They sometimes fought each other, or people who lived farther west, but they had plenty of food and traded with villages hundreds of miles away. Soon, however, the arrival of a new and distant people would change their way of life forever.

# READ ABOUT

Giovanni da
Verrazzano's ship
entering Newport
Harbor, 1524

**1524**
*Giovanni da Verrazzano becomes the first European known to reach Rhode Island*

▲ **1636**
*Roger Williams settles in Providence*

**1663**
*Rhode Island receives a charter from King Charles II of England*

## CHAPTER THREE

# EXPLORATION AND SETTLEMENT

★

ONE DAY IN 1524, WAMPANOAGS IN SMALL BOATS APPROACHED A VESSEL THAT HAD SAILED INTO NARRAGANSETT BAY. From the huge ship, strangely dressed sailors tossed down bells and other small items to the people in the canoes. Sensing the newcomers were friendly, the Native Americans invited them to their village. This pleasant meeting marked the first known arrival of Europeans in the region.

**1675**
King Philip's War erupts
between Native Americans
and European settlers

**1772**
Colonists burn the
British ship Gaspee

**1790 ▲**
Rhode Island becomes
the 13th state to ratify
the U.S. Constitution

# European Exploration of Rhode Island

The colored arrows on this map show the routes taken by European explorers from 1524 to 1614.

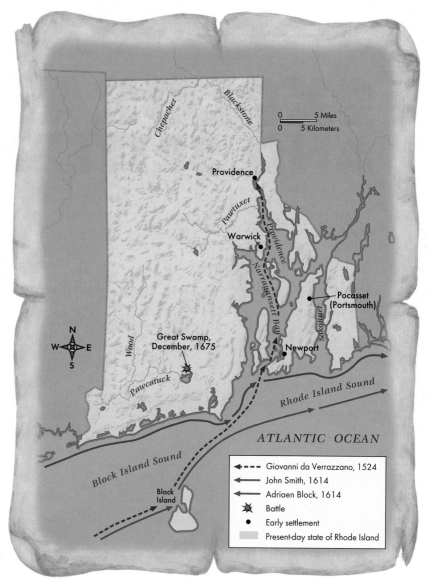

0 — 5 Miles
0 — 5 Kilometers

Chepachet

Blackstone

Providence

Pawtuxet

Warwick

Providence

Narragansett Bay

Pocasset
(Portsmouth)

Sakonnet

N
W          E
S

Wood

Great Swamp,
December, 1675

Newport

Pawcatuck

Rhode Island Sound

ATLANTIC OCEAN

Block Island Sound

Block
Island

◄---- Giovanni da Verrazzano, 1524
◄—— John Smith, 1614
◄—— Adriaen Block, 1614
✸ Battle
● Early settlement
▢ Present-day state of Rhode Island

## WORD TO KNOW

**colonies** *communities settled in a new land but with ties to another government*

## EUROPEAN EXPLORERS

The captain of the ship that reached Rhode Island in 1524 was Giovanni da Verrazzano. He was an Italian sailing for France, which was competing with other European nations to gain **colonies** in the Americas. Since the voyages of Christopher Columbus during the 1490s, Europeans had looked to North and South America for gold and a western

European settlers building a ship in Narragansett Bay, early 1600s

route to China. After Verrazzano's visit, almost 100 years passed before other foreign explorers sailed past Rhode Island or entered its bay.

In 1614, English explorer John Smith sailed all along the New England coast. He drew maps and wrote letters that described its natural beauty. He hoped English settlers would start colonies in the region. The same year, Dutch sea captain Adriaen Block sailed across Long Island Sound. He named an island he saw after himself—Block Island. Neither Smith nor Block actually came ashore in what is now Rhode Island, but just a few years later, English colonists began settling to the north, in Massachusetts. Their settlements—and arguments— would shape the growth of Rhode Island.

As depicted here from a European perspective, Roger Williams was greeted by Native people upon his arrival in Rhode Island.

## RELIGIOUS CHANGES

For many centuries, the Roman Catholic Church was the only Christian faith in western Europe. Starting in the early 1500s, however, some people began questioning Catholic practices and founding other churches. They became known as Protestants.

In 1534, England's King Henry VIII broke away from the Catholic Church and started the Church of England. Over the decades, some English Protestants thought the new church did not go far enough in getting rid of Catholic teachings. These Protestants became known as Puritans, because they wanted to purify the Church of England. Other Protestants thought the Church of England could never be a true Christian church. They wanted to separate from it completely, and they became known as Separatists.

In 1620, a group of Separatists left England to form their own colony in Massachusetts, where they could worship as they chose. The Separatists landed in Plymouth, and today they are sometimes called the Pilgrims. In the years that followed, many Puritans left England for Massachusetts. They settled in what are now Salem and Boston and called their colony Massachusetts Bay.

## ROGER WILLIAMS ARRIVES

Roger Williams was one of several thousand Puritans who came to Massachusetts Bay during the 1630s. He was a minister, and he took a job at the church in Salem. Soon, however, Williams upset some colonial leaders. He was more of a Separatist than a Puritan. He believed that the government should not dictate a person's religious actions or beliefs. The Puritans ran both the church and the government, and they punished people who did not go to church. Williams believed each person should be allowed to decide what religion to follow. "Forced religion," he said, "stinks in the nostrils of God."

For several years, Williams bounced from town to town in Massachusetts Bay and Plymouth. He angered leaders by attacking Puritan practices. He also stated that England had no legal right to claim land in New England. The land, he said, belonged to the Algonquian people. Fed up with Williams and his ideas, the leaders of Massachusetts Bay **banished** him from the colony. Before he could be sent back to England, Williams fled south, to the land of the Wampanoag Nation.

The Wampanoag people agreed to sell Williams land near the Seekonk River, so he could start a **plantation**. The leaders of Plymouth, however, thought he was too close to their colony, so they asked him to move. He and a few followers then bought land from the Narragansett Nation, at

## WORDS TO KNOW

**banished** *sent out of a place forever*

**plantation** *a large farm that grows mainly one crop*

**Q8 WHO WAS RHODE ISLAND'S FIRST EUROPEAN SETTLER?**

**A8** William Blackstone was the first European to live in Rhode Island. He moved to Massachusetts in 1623 and then to Rhode Island in 1635, settling in what is now Cumberland. The Blackstone River, which cuts through northeastern Rhode Island, is named for him.

a spot where the Mosshasuck and Woonasquatucket rivers meet. Williams called his new settlement Providence.

Williams had good relations with the Algonquian people. Unlike other Puritan settlers, he respected their right to have their own religion, though he did try to teach them Christian beliefs. He purchased land, while other Europeans tried to take it by force. His friends included Canonicus and Miantonomi, two Narragansett sachems, or leaders. Williams convinced the Narragansett Nation not to join the Pequot people in a war against Puritans in Massachusetts and Connecticut in 1636.

## NEW TOWNS

Religious disagreements also prompted other Puritans to leave Massachusetts Bay for Rhode Island. Anne Hutchinson upset Puritan leaders when she challenged their religious authority. Like Williams, she was banished. She moved to Providence in 1638, and with Williams's help, she and her supporters bought Aquidneck Island from the Narragansett people. They called their settlement Pocasset, though they renamed it Portsmouth a few years later. They also renamed their island Rhode Island.

The settlers in Portsmouth included William Coddington. Because of a political dispute, Coddington started a new town on the southern end of the island in 1639. He called it Newport. By the end of the year, almost 100 people lived there.

Another Portsmouth resident who set out on his own was Samuel Gorton. He had been banished from Plymouth, but his beliefs upset leaders in Portsmouth. Gorton said men and women were completely equal—an uncommon idea at the time. Banished from Portsmouth, Gorton went to Providence before starting a new town, Warwick.

## THE CHARTER

The first Rhode Islanders argued over more than just religion. Some Providence settlers wanted more land for themselves, so they split off to form the town of Pawtuxet. The leaders there upset Williams and others when they declared their loyalty to Massachusetts. Williams knew his Providence Plantation and the other settlements nearby did not have a legal right to exist. Unlike Plymouth and Massachusetts Bay, they didn't have a **charter** from England. To make sure

### WORD TO KNOW

**charter** *a document from a ruler granting rights to a group*

## ANNE HUTCHINSON: A DARING WOMAN

Anne Hutchinson (1591–1643) and her family reached Boston from England in 1634. Soon she was challenging the local Puritans with her religious ideas. She said a good Christian did not have to follow the rules of a church or of society to go to heaven. Direct, spiritual contact with God was all a believer needed. She was tried before a civil court for teaching her ideas in Boston and was forced out of Massachusetts Bay. After she and her followers founded Portsmouth, Hutchinson moved in 1642 to Long Island, New York. She was killed there the next year during a conflict with Native Americans.

 **Want to know more?** Visit www.factsfornow .scholastic.com and enter the keywords **Rhode Island**.

A view of Portsmouth in 1638

Rhode Island colonists welcomed Roger Williams when he returned with the colonial charter in 1644.

## WORD TO KNOW

**Parliament** *the legislature in Great Britain*

Massachusetts leaders left the Rhode Islanders alone, Williams sailed to England in 1643 to obtain a charter.

At the time, England was in the middle of a civil war. King Charles I was fighting the Puritans who controlled **Parliament**. Williams received a charter from Parliament, which united Providence, Newport, and Portsmouth. Warwick joined the next year, and Pawtuxet became a part of Providence again about a decade later. The charter gave Rhode Islanders the right to run their own local governments. However, the charter didn't spell out the new colony's borders, and this led to decades of conflicts with neighboring Massachusetts Bay and Connecticut.

Still, the colony continued to grow. Its practice of allowing everyone to worship freely drew Quakers,

Baptists, and other Protestants who rejected Puritan beliefs. Some Jewish people also began settling in the colony during the 1650s.

## LIFE IN THE COLONY

The first settlers in Rhode Island raised corn and beans, crops they had learned about from the Algonquians. The settlers also grew crops they had brought with them from England, such as apples, peas, carrots, and barley. Like the neighboring Indians, the settlers also ate fish from Narragansett Bay and hunted deer and other game. The Rhode Island colonists lived in small wooden houses, though over time the richest settlers built larger homes. Cattle, sheep, and other livestock grazed on the islands of Narragansett Bay. On Aquidneck Island, William Coddington and other wealthy settlers started large farms and hired others to work them. Later, other plantations appeared west of the bay, from Charlestown to Warwick.

The Atlantic Ocean also provided jobs and wealth for Rhode Islanders. Starting around 1670, shipbuilding became a major industry. Rhode Island merchants used these ships to bring farm goods to Boston and to islands in the Caribbean. Newport became a favorite stopping point for pirates who sailed the Atlantic and the Caribbean. The presence of pirates, other criminals, and people with unusual religious views led some New Englanders to call Rhode Island "**Rogue**'s Island."

## NEW CHALLENGES

Although Rhode Islanders had freedom to worship as they chose, they were still tied to Great Britain. In 1661, Puritans in Great Britain lost power and Charles II became king. Williams and others worried that the king might not honor Rhode Island's charter of 1643.

**William Coddington**

Captain Kidd, a pirate who visited Rhode Island, may have left buried treasure there. Some folks claim that he left his loot on Block Island or on an island in Narragansett Bay. But no riches have ever been found.

## WORD TO KNOW

**rogue** *a dishonest or worthless person*

However, Reverend John Clarke, a resident of the Rhode Island colony, worked with King Charles II to secure a new charter. The charter was granted in 1663, creating the "colony of Rhode Island and Providence Plantations" and providing religious freedom for all. Rhode Islanders could control their local government, as long as their laws did not violate England's. However, the charter did not solve Rhode Island's border disputes with its neighbors. The current boundaries of Rhode Island were not set until 1747.

## KING PHILIP'S WAR

Since the arrival of Roger Williams, life had been mostly peaceful in Rhode Island, thanks to Williams's honest dealings with the Algonquian leaders. But the peace was shattered in 1675, when a war between Massachusetts settlers and the Wampanoag Nation spread into Rhode Island.

The death of Wamsutta, brother of Metacomet

The Wampanoag sachem was named Metacomet, but the English called him King Philip, and the war was named for him. Metacomet went to war after his brother, Wamsutta, died following hours of questioning by the English. The Narragansett people entered the war after Plymouth settlers attacked their camp.

King Philip's War spread across southern New England. During the war, Providence burned, and more than 50 other English towns were attacked. At the same time, several women emerged as Native American leaders. Ashawonks, a leader of the Sakonnet Indians, sided with Metacomet for a time but later made a peace agreement with the European settlers. Another Algonquian woman leader during the war was Wetamoo, who was married to Wamsutta. As the colonists pursued her and her people in 1676, Wetamoo drowned trying to escape across the Fall River.

The settlers won the war in the summer of 1676. With their defeat, many Wampanoags and Narragansetts were sold into slavery, including Metacomet's wife and son. King Philip's War marked the last major Indian war in southern New England. The remaining Wampanoags and Narragansetts in Rhode Island were forced to live on a small piece of land near Charlestown. Over time, they lost more and more of this land and struggled to survive. Many took jobs working for settlers.

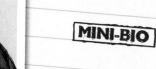

**MINI-BIO**

## METACOMET: DEFENDER OF HIS PEOPLE

Metacomet (1639?–1676) was the son of Massasoit, the Wampanoag sachem who had welcomed the Pilgrims when they landed in Plymouth. By the time Metacomet took over as sachem in 1662, the Wampanoag Nation had lost much of its land to the newcomers. In 1675, Metacomet fought the English to preserve what was left of Indian land and culture. During King Philip's War, Metacomet rode a black horse, a gift from the English during friendlier days. He rode as far as New York to escape capture, before returning to his camp in Bristol, Rhode Island, where he was killed by a Native American working for the English.

**? Want to know more?** Visit www.factsfor now.scholastic.com and enter the keywords **Rhode Island**.

In the 1700s, ships sailed in and out of Rhode Island's busy ports.

## TIME OF GROWTH

During the 18th century, Rhode Island's population grew dramatically. In 1690, about 4,000 people lived in the colony; by 1755, Rhode Island was home to 42,000. Trade and shipping helped fuel the economy. Rhode Island ships carried livestock, candles, fish, cheese, and rum (an alcoholic drink) to merchants in the southern colonies, the Caribbean, and Africa. The ships returned with sugar, molasses, goods from England—and enslaved Africans. During most of the 18th century, the slave trade made Rhode Island merchants such as the Brown and the Lopez families very wealthy. Rhode Island traders controlled between 60 percent and 90 percent of the entire slave trade with the English colonies.

Sea captains from Newport and Bristol traveled to West Africa, where they traded rum for kidnapped Africans. On the long voyage from Africa to North America, as many as 20 percent of the slaves died from the brutal, crowded, and filthy conditions on the slave ships.

## SLAVERY IN RHODE ISLAND

During most of the 17th century, farmers and others in Rhode Island who needed help usually hired servants. Many servants signed a contract called an indenture. The servant promised to work for a master for a set number of years. In return, masters gave their indentured servants food, clothing, and a place to live. Most indentured servants came from Great Britain, but some Africans also became indentured servants. They were free to leave their masters after 10 years.

Enslaved Africans, however, did not have that freedom. Slaves had lived in Rhode Island almost from the time the colony was founded. Native Americans were the first enslaved people in the colony. They were usually women and children captured after the Native American men had been killed.

Starting in the early 1700s, some of the enslaved people whom Rhode Island traders had brought from Africa ended up in Rhode Island. By 1708, slaves outnumbered white indentured servants in the colony by almost 8 to 1. By 1755, enslaved Africans made up 11.5 percent of the population of Rhode Island.

In the southern part of the state, enslaved Africans tended cattle and sheep and worked on dairy farms. In the northern part, they worked as house servants, crafts-

## PIONEERING EDUCATOR

Sarah Osborn (1714–1796) was a pioneering Rhode Island reformer who believed that slavery should be abolished and that Africans and women deserved an education, just like white men. She supported herself as a teacher and then began a school in Newport. In the 1760s, her school had both male and female students, even though at the time most women did not receive formal educations. She also conducted religious discussions every night in her home. In a given week, she spoke to 500 men, women, and children, black and white. In the 1770s, she became ill, and her educational work was taken up by leading Newport ministers, who also promoted the idea that slavery should be abolished.

## FAQ

### Q8 WHO WAS THE BLACK "GOVERNOR" OF RHODE ISLAND?

**A8** White masters allowed enslaved Africans to have an "election day" in which they would elect one person as their so-called governor. The governor was respected among the enslaved people, and he had the power to punish slaves who harmed other slaves. But he had no legal power over white Rhode Islanders. Election Day became a huge celebration, with music and food.

## WORD TO KNOW

**smuggle** *to bring in or take out illegally*

people, and sailors. Enslaved people in Rhode Island had some legal rights. Some had a chance to earn money, and a few were able to buy their freedom. They could testify in court against white people and challenge jurors in their own cases. Enslaved people in the southern colonies lacked these rights. Still, enslaved Africans often tried to escape. Many ran away with enslaved Indians or with white indentured servants. So many people ran away that as early as 1710, the colony's laws called for severely punishing escaped slaves who were caught and any whites who helped them.

## THE ROAD TO REVOLUTION

Starting at the end of the 17th century, Great Britain and France fought several wars as they competed to control North America. The last of these, called the French and Indian War (1754–63), ended with a British victory, giving that country almost all of France's lands east of the Mississippi River. Soon after the war, King George III decided Great Britain needed to raise money in the colonies to pay its debts and keep soldiers in North America.

In 1764, Great Britain passed the Sugar Act. This law made it harder for Rhode Islanders to **smuggle** molasses and sugar from the West Indies, as they had in the past, to avoid paying taxes. More British ships patrolled Narragansett Bay, and smugglers who were caught faced trial outside the colony. The British action threatened to destroy the colony's rum industry. Governor Stephen Hopkins was one of the first Americans to protest taxes on the colonies. He said Parliament did not have a right to tax them because the Americans had no elected officials representing their interests.

Anger over British policies grew the next year, when Parliament passed the Stamp Act. The law placed a tax

The burning of the *Gaspee*, a British
ship, in Narragansett Bay, 1772

on paper goods and documents used in the colonies.
Mobs stormed the homes of three Rhode Islanders who
supported the king. The British did not enforce the new
law, but in the following years they passed other taxes
on the colonies. In Newport, tensions rose when the
British forced local sailors to work on their ships. The
bad feelings grew in 1772, when some Providence residents burned the *Gaspee*, a British naval ship, after it ran
aground near Warwick.

**The first circus in the American
colonies was founded in
Newport in 1774. It featured
trick horse-riding.**

Patriot troops carrying gunpowder near Portsmouth, 1775

## BATTLE FOR INDEPENDENCE

In April 1775, British troops stationed in Boston clashed with Massachusetts **patriots**. Their battles marked the start of the American Revolution. Rhode Island soon sent troops to help fight the British, though some local residents did remain loyal to the king. In June 1775, a small Rhode Island fleet captured a British ship, and local **privateers** captured many more ships throughout the war.

On May 4, 1776, Rhode Island became the first colony to declare independence from Great Britain. In July, the United States as a whole officially declared its independence. Patriots in Newport celebrated the news, but the cheering was over by December, when the British took over the city and other parts of southern Rhode Island. British troops raided local farms for food, cut down trees for firewood, and burned many homes.

# Rhode Island:
# From Territory to Statehood
## (1763–1790)

This map shows many of the colonies and the area that became the state of Rhode Island in 1790.

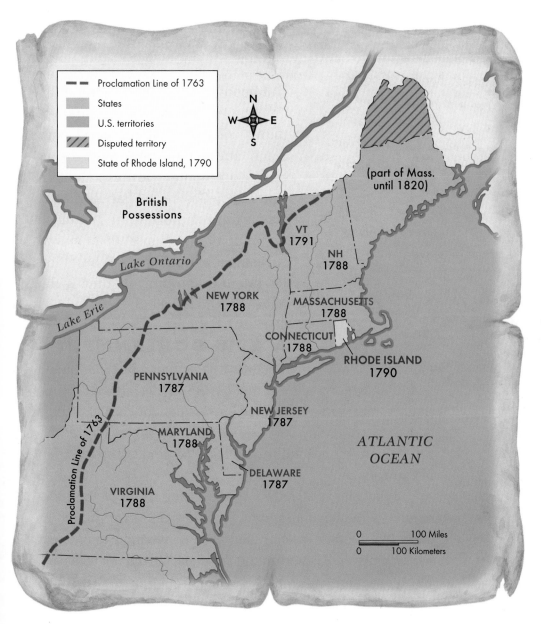

Proclamation Line of 1763
States
U.S. territories
Disputed territory
State of Rhode Island, 1790

N
W E
S

British
Possessions

Lake Ontario

Lake Erie

(part of Mass.
until 1820)

VT
1791

NH
1788

NEW YORK
1788

MASSACHUSETTS
1788

CONNECTICUT
1788

RHODE ISLAND
1790

PENNSYLVANIA
1787

NEW JERSEY
1787

Proclamation Line of 1763

MARYLAND
1788

DELAWARE
1787

ATLANTIC
OCEAN

VIRGINIA
1788

0          100 Miles
0      100 Kilometers

## NATHANAEL GREENE: PATRIOT

During the revolution, no Rhode Islander did more for the American cause than Nathanael Greene (1742–1786). Born in Warwick, he had no military experience when he was named a major general in 1776. But he strongly supported the struggle for independence and eagerly did whatever he could to help. For a time, he located food and supplies for the troops. His greatest fame, however, came on the battlefield, where he led the Americans to victory in several key battles in the South. After the war, Georgia rewarded him for his efforts by giving him land, and he died in that state.

**? Want to know more?** Visit www.factsfor now.scholastic.com and enter the keywords **Rhode Island**.

## WOW

**The largest land battle of the American Revolution in New England took place near Newport in August 1778. Between 12,000 and 15,000 soldiers took part in the Battle of Rhode Island.**

To fight back, some Rhode Islanders carried out a daring raid of their own. On July 9, 1777, Colonel William Barton led a group of men who captured British general George Prescott from a house in Portsmouth where he sometimes stayed. The Americans later swapped Prescott for one of their own generals who had been captured by the British.

Rhode Island was one of many colonies that recruited both black and white men to fight in the Continental army. General Nathanael Greene's First Regiment was a unit of more than 120 black men, including almost 100 enslaved Africans. Members of the First Regiment fought bravely during the Battle of Rhode Island.

## A NEW GOVERNMENT

The war finally ended in 1783. Rhode Island was now one of the 13 U.S. states. Its residents, though, had paid a high price for independence. The British had devastated Newport, Rhode Island's largest city at the time. Several thousand people had fled, and many resettled in Providence.

Many Rhode Islanders feared losing some of the independence they had just won to the new U.S. government. In 1787, when other states called for a convention to create a stronger national government, Rhode Island did not take part. The convention ended with the drafting of the **Constitution**, which created the U.S. government still used today.

As the other states began to ratify, or approve, the Constitution, Rhode Island lawmakers refused to consider it. James Madison, who helped write the Constitution, once complained about the "wickedness and folly" that seemed to grip Rhode Island's leaders. But many Rhode Island business owners liked the fact that the new national government was going to pay state debts from the war. Finally, in 1790, the state's merchants and a visit from George Washington, who had led the Continental army during the war, convinced the state's lawmakers to ratify the Constitution. Rhode Island was now the 13th state in the Union.

This map of the Battle of Rhode Island shows the position of French ships and the American army under the command of General John Sullivan in 1778.

## WORD TO KNOW

**Constitution** *the written document that contains all the governing principles of the United States*

48

Providence in 1827

▲ **1793**
*Samuel Slater opens the
first mechanized textile
mill in the United States*

**1833**
*Workers begin
building a railroad
across the state*

**1841**
*Thomas Dorr leads
a rebellion over
voting rights*

# CHAPTER FOUR

# GROWTH AND CHANGE

★

THE RUSH OF WATER OVER A WOODEN WHEEL, THE HUM OF MACHINES—THESE WERE THE SOUNDS OF RHODE ISLAND IN THE EARLY 19TH CENTURY. The state became a national leader in building mills and factories, and it attracted many thousands of immigrants to work in them.

**1860s ▶**
Elizabeth Buffum
Chace harbors
runaway slaves

**1888**
*The law is changed so
that immigrants can vote
in statewide elections
without owning property*

**1917**
*Thousands of Rhode
Islanders join the military
to fight in World War I*

## PIONEERING ACTIVIST

Occramar Marycoo (1746–1826) was a teenager when he left his native Ghana for North America. A sea captain had promised to take the young African there so he could go to school. Instead, the captain sold Marycoo into slavery in Rhode Island, and the teen was renamed Newport Gardner. In Newport, he used his skills as a musician to earn money and buy his freedom. He continued his musical career, but he also worked hard to help other free Africans. In 1780, he started the African Union Society, and later he started a school for black children and Newport's first church for blacks. Gardner, however, lost faith that Africans would ever receive equal treatment in the United States, and he returned to Africa shortly before his death.

## NEW WAYS TO WEALTH

After the American Revolution, Rhode Island granted several hundred enslaved Africans their freedom for fighting in the war. It also passed a law that children born to slaves after March 1, 1784, would be free. Then, in 1787, a state law ended the slave trade. Rhode Island merchants, however, were not willing to end their trade in slaves. Some sailed to and from ports in other states, and others smuggled slaves. The wealthy Brown family of Providence was deeply divided over the slave trade. Moses Brown took his brother John to court because he continued to bring slaves to the state.

Shippers who didn't want to break the law found a booming business trading goods in China and other parts of Asia. They brought back items such as tea, coffee, silk, china dishes, and fabrics. Robert Gray of Tiverton led the way, reaching China in 1789. His ship, the *Columbia Rediviva*, became the first American vessel to sail completely around the world when it returned to New England.

After 1790, however, a new industry offered investors another way to make money. That year, Samuel Slater arrived in Rhode Island from England. He came with plans for building the most advanced spinning machine of the day. Until then, only the British used the machines to spin cotton thread. The rest of the world still did the job by hand. Moses Brown and his partner invested money so Slater could build a textile factory in Pawtucket, the first ever in the United States. It opened in 1793, and others soon followed. The rivers in the northeastern corner of Rhode Island powered waterwheels that turned the machines in the factories. By 1815, the state had 100 cotton mills, and wool mills soon opened, too. Steam engines slowly replaced waterwheels as the mills' source of power. With these factories, the American Industrial Revolution was born.

This cotton mill was established on the Blackstone River by Samuel Slater in 1793.

## ANOTHER WAR

As Rhode Island began to industrialize, more trouble was brewing. Wars between France and Great Britain affected American shippers. The Americans wanted to trade with both sides, but the French and British did not want them trading with their enemy. The situation finally led to the War of 1812, another war between the United States and Great Britain. Most Rhode Islanders opposed the war, because they made most

**FAQ**

**Q:** WHAT WAS THE INDUSTRIAL REVOLUTION?

**A:** The Industrial Revolution was a period when industry replaced farming as the main source of jobs. It began in the 18th century in England. During the Industrial Revolution, waterpower, steam engines, and finally electric- and gas-powered engines replaced animals and humans as the main source of power for most tasks.

It was not unusual for children to work long hours in textile mills in Rhode Island and other states.

of their money trading with the British. In 1814, some even talked about joining the other New England states in leaving the Union. But Rhode Island remained a state, and the war ended in 1815.

## AN INDUSTRIAL STATE

In the two decades after the War of 1812, more Rhode Island investors turned to manufacturing. In addition to producing textiles, state workers crafted the spinning machines and looms used in the factories in Rhode Island and other states. The state also became a center for making jewelry and silver goods. Providence became the financial and transportation center of the state.

As more money went into building factories in Rhode Island, the shipping trade almost completely dried up. Newport and other coastal towns lost jobs. Farming also became less important, as people left the land to work in the mills.

Many of the textile workers were women and children. Millwork gave young women their first chance to leave their small towns and have some independence. But in the mills, they faced long hours and dangerous work conditions for low pay. Children suffered even more from millwork. Rhode Island's first public school system began in the 1820s, but many children went to the mills rather than school. They needed to make money for their families. In some textile mills, half the workers were children.

The rise of industry also brought many immigrants to Rhode Island. The Irish started coming in the 1820s. They worked in the mills and helped build the Blackstone Canal, which connected Providence to the industrial city of Worcester, Massachusetts. Starting in 1833, they also worked building railroads in the state. During the 1860s, French Canadians began heading south to Rhode Island. Like the Irish, they were mostly Roman Catholic, while most native-born Rhode Islanders were Protestant. Because of this, the new arrivals sometimes faced **prejudice**. Many companies ran ads saying "No Irish need apply." The French Canadians also struggled to fit in because they didn't speak English.

Narragansetts who remained in the state also faced prejudice. For several decades, they had not been allowed to run their own government on their lands in Charlestown. And white Americans expected them to give up their traditional culture and live as whites did.

Prejudice against African Americans was even stronger. In 1822, a state law barred them from voting, and in 1824 and 1831, whites rioted against peaceful black communities. In Providence, the black community fought back against the rioters.

## WOW

In 1824, textile mill workers in Pawtucket went on **strike** when mill owners tried to cut wages by 25 percent. Never before had women taken part in a strike in the United States.

## WORDS TO KNOW

**strike** *an organized refusal to work, usually as a sign of protest about working conditions*

**prejudice** *an unreasonable hatred or fear of others*

## THE DORR REBELLION

Immigration and a changing economy led to political troubles in Rhode Island. In the 1840s, the charter of 1663 was still the supreme law of the state. Unlike the other colonies, Rhode Island had not written a constitution when it became a state. The charter limited voting to male landowners, making Rhode Island one of few states that still did not allow all white men to vote. This upset many Rhode Islanders. Most immigrants and mill workers didn't own land, so they couldn't vote. The voting restrictions also affected merchants and artisans whose jobs didn't require land.

Because of these rules, more than half of the adult white men in Rhode Island could not vote. Free blacks had lost the right to vote in 1822, and women could not vote either. The charter also gave the state's rural towns vastly greater representation in the General Assembly, the state's lawmaking body, than the rapidly growing towns in the industrial corner of the state.

Some Rhode Islanders began to demand an end to these unfair arrangements, and Thomas Dorr, a wealthy lawyer and lawmaker, emerged as their leader. Dorr's supporters formed the People's Party and held statewide elections. Dorr was elected governor. In 1841, he and his supporters drafted their own constitution that would have allowed all white men to vote.

Meanwhile, Samuel Ward King of the Law and Order Party was elected governor under the charter. For a time, the state had two elected governments. Dorr's was illegal, but it had the support of many Rhode Islanders. In 1842, supporters of the People's Party prepared to fight sup-

Thomas
Dorr

porters of the Law and Order Party. Dorr led an assault on the Providence arsenal, where weapons were stored. The attack failed, and Dorr briefly fled the state.

The so-called Dorr Rebellion ended when the Law and Order Party wrote a constitution in 1843. Under this constitution, native-born men, both black and white, were allowed to vote without owning property. This constitution also gave cities more members in the General Assembly, the state's lawmaking body. Immigrants, however, still faced severe limits on their voting rights. Foreign-born U.S. citizens who did not own property could not vote in state or national elections.

Samuel Ward King issued this proclamation calling Thomas Dorr a traitor.

## THE CIVIL WAR

By 1860, the United States was deeply divided over the issue of slavery. Many Southerners, even some who did not own slaves, believed slavery was necessary to keep their plantations and businesses running. Many Northerners opposed the spread of slavery into new states and territories, and a smaller number were abolitionists, people who wanted to end slavery entirely. Elizabeth Buffum Chace of Smithfield harbored runaway slaves and helped organize an antislavery society. But Rhode Island textile mills used Southern cotton as their raw material, and some Southerners vacationed in Newport. With those ties, the state did not have a strong abolitionist movement.

However, when Southern states began leaving the Union in December 1860, sparking the Civil War, Rhode

Colonel Ambrose Burnside (seated center) and members of the 1st Rhode Island Infantry Regiment in 1861

**FAQ**

### Q8 WHAT IS AMBROSE BURNSIDE BEST KNOWN FOR?

**A8** Burnside grew long tufts of hair on either side of his face. After the Civil War, similar facial hair was called "sideburns" in his honor, and the term is still used today.

Islanders wanted to keep the Union whole. When the actual fighting began the next April, young Rhode Island men of both races volunteered to fight for the Union. About 1,800 African American Rhode Islanders fought in all-black units with white officers.

Rhode Island resident Ambrose Burnside rose to the rank of general and led Union troops at several key battles. Governor William Sprague also served as an officer. And Kady Brownell was one of a handful of women who fought during the Civil War. Brownell followed her husband from Providence to the battlefield and trained with the soldiers. She was the only woman to receive discharge papers from the government after her military service. But she represented the kind of service thousands of New England women were ready to offer to ensure a Union victory.

## BOOM TIMES

The Civil War ended in 1865 with a Northern victory. Rhode Islanders went back to work in the state's many textile mills and other factories. The men who owned the factories continued to control Rhode Island politics, and **corruption** was common. Party leaders paid voters to elect their candidates, and some state officials used their positions to make money illegally. The idea of Rhode Island as "Rogue's Island" continued.

But the war had also been a time of racial progress. When the war started, Providence, Newport, and Bristol still sent blacks and whites to separate schools. Less than six months after the war ended, Newport **integrated** its schools. Then in 1866, the state integrated all its schools.

In the decades after the Civil War, Rhode Island became a popular vacation spot for wealthy people from across the East. With its rich sailing heritage, Rhode Island also became a center for building and sailing pleasure boats. Newport drew the richest of the rich, and some built huge mansions they called "cottages." Westerly, Jamestown, Narragansett, and Block Island also attracted tourists, not all of them wealthy. Coastal towns built amusement parks and boardwalks for average people looking for fun on their day off from work. Lighthouses were constructed along the coast to keep boaters safe.

### ELIZABETH BUFFUM CHACE: A FIGHTER FOR RIGHTS

Elizabeth Buffum Chace (1806–1899) was a Quaker, a member of a Christian group that supported the idea that all people are equal. The Smithfield native married a wealthy cotton mill owner and then spent decades campaigning to end slavery and help women gain the right to vote. She also worked to improve conditions in women's prisons and helped start a school for homeless children. In 2001, Rhode Island put a statue of Chace in the capitol, making her the first woman to receive that honor.

**?** **Want to know more?** Visit www.factsfornow.scholastic.com and enter the keywords **Rhode Island**.

### WORDS TO KNOW

**corruption** *illegal or unfair acts committed by government or business officials*

**integrated** *brought together all members of society*

## THE BREAKERS

Of all the grand Newport mansions, none was grander than the Breakers. The stone home was built by Cornelius Vanderbilt II, whose family had made a fortune in steamships and railroads. In 1893, work began on the house, which was modeled after 16th-century Italian mansions. When it was done, the Breakers featured 70 rooms, including a "great hall" with ceilings 45 feet (14 m) high. Visitors to Newport can tour this and other nearby mansions.

**MINI-BIO**

## IDA LEWIS: LIGHTHOUSE KEEPER

Ida Lewis (1842–1911), who was born in Newport, was the keeper of the Lime Rock Lighthouse in Newport Harbor for nearly 50 years. During that time, she rescued at least 17 people, including six soldiers, from drowning. Her father had been the lighthouse keeper, and she took over unofficially after he became ill in the late 1850s. The government did not make her the official keeper until 1879. Two years later, she received a medal from the U.S. Lighthouse Service for her heroics.

**? Want to know more?** Visit www.factsfor now.scholastic.com and enter the keywords **Rhode Island**.

The Breakers mansion in Newport

An Italian family inside their home in Providence, late 1800s

## NEW ARRIVALS, OLD PROBLEMS

With Rhode Island's many factories constantly humming, more immigrants came to the state looking for jobs. French Canadians continued to flock there, taking unskilled jobs in mills. Skilled textile workers from the British Isles often managed the mills. After 1880, more immigrants arrived from Italy, Portugal, Poland, and eastern Europe. The constant stream of immigrants helped push the population of Providence from 54,595 in 1865 to 175,597 in 1900. Pawtucket and Woonsocket were also thriving factory cities. Thousands of people arrived on vessels owned by the Fabre Line, a French shipping company.

Newcomers continued to face restrictions on voting. In 1888, an amendment, or change, to the state constitution finally gave immigrants the right to vote for city mayors and in national and statewide elections, even if they didn't own property. But no one who lived in a city—natives or immigrants—could vote for local lawmakers unless they owned property. About 60 percent of Rhode Island's city residents were thereby shut out of local elections.

Other laws gave the state senate the power to choose most nonelected government officials. The senate still gave rural towns more power than cities, where most immigrants lived. For the first few decades of the 20th century, businesses and rural residents controlled Rhode Island politics, shutting out factory workers and immigrants.

The state's first settlers, the Narragansett people, also struggled in these years. In 1880, the state said the Narragansett Nation was no longer an official tribe, so state residents could start buying Narragansett lands. The remaining Narragansett people began taking jobs and living in nearby towns, but they never stopped their fight to regain their lands.

These members of the Rhode Island Women's League, photographed in 1900, fought for voting rights and other women's issues.

Navy recruits boarding a train in Newport, 1917

## A WORLD AT WAR

By the early 1900s, the Rhode Island economy began to lose some steam. Companies could make textiles cheaper in southern states, where wages were lower.

In 1917, the United States entered World War I, which was already raging in Europe. The United States joined on the side of Great Britain, France, and other nations that were fighting Germany and its **allies**. Thousands of Rhode Islanders soon found jobs working for the U.S. government or companies that supplied the troops. The government trained sailors for merchant ships in Newport, and Goat Island was the home of the Naval Torpedo Station. Several thousand workers there, including 300 women, helped build weapons to destroy German submarines.

The war ended with a German defeat in 1918. Rhode Islanders hoped for better days to come.

## WORD TO KNOW

**allies** *people who are on the same side in a conflict*

# READ ABOUT

Men and boys prepare to start their workday at the Warren Manufacturing Company, early 1900s

## 1922

*Isabelle Ahearn O'Neill becomes the first female lawmaker in Rhode Island*

## 1933 ▲

*Theodore Francis Green is elected governor and later takes part in the Bloodless Revolution*

## 1950

*Providence is home to nearly 250,000 people*

MORE MODERN TIMES

CHAPTER FIVE

# MORE MODERN TIMES

★

I N THE 1920s, MOST OF THE COUNTRY ENJOYED THE ROARING TWENTIES. As the U.S. economy boomed, people danced to jazz music, listened to the first radios, and watched the first films with sound. But for Rhode Island, the 1920s were more of a whimper than a roar. Industries struggled, and politicians battled. The rogues still seemed to be in control.

**▲1978**
*The Narragansett Nation wins back its land in Charlestown*

**1980–2000**
*Rhode Island's Hispanic population quadruples*

**2010**
*Flooding forces thousands of people from their homes*

**MINI-BIO**

## THEODORE FRANCIS GREEN: "REVOLUTIONARY" GOVERNOR

Theodore Francis Green (1867–1966) was a rarity in Rhode Island politics: a wealthy, white Protestant who was also a Democrat. He was elected governor in 1933, and in 1935 he took part in what has been called the Bloodless Revolution. Green and his supporters managed to overturn the election of two Republicans to the state senate. Their success gave the Democrats control of both houses in the General Assembly, and they soon filled the state supreme court and other parts of the state government with Democrats. These moves gave the Democrats control over Rhode Island politics for years to come. After serving as governor, Green represented Rhode Island in the U.S. Senate for 24 years.

**? Want to know more?** Visit www.factsfornow .scholastic.com and enter the keywords **Rhode Island**.

**W★W**

Politics was sometimes dirty in Rhode Island—and smelly too! In 1924, Republicans hired a crook to set off a stink bomb in the General Assembly, hoping to end a debate on an issue important to the Democrats.

## TOUGH TIMES

After World War I, Rhode Island's textile industry continued its decline. Companies fired workers, cut wages, or shut down completely. At times, workers went on strike to demand better pay, but the industry was dying in the state where it had been born. And few new companies appeared to replace the lost jobs.

Throughout these years, Rhode Island's political leaders squabbled with each other. The Republican Party had controlled the state for decades, but during the 1920s, Democrats won the support of immigrant voters and began to take over. They managed to give larger towns more representatives in the state senate. They also finally ended the property requirement to vote in local elections. With that change, the Democrats were able to win many elections in cities and towns. During the 1930s, many Democrats of Irish, French Canadian, and Italian descent got government positions, replacing Republicans with British roots.

In 1935, Governor Theodore Francis Green solidified Democratic control in what became known as the Bloodless Revolution. Green replaced all the Republicans on the state supreme court and replaced many other Republican government appointees. Since that time, Democrats have been the dominant party in the state.

Mill workers on strike in Pawtucket, 1922

## FROM BAD TO WORSE

In 1929, the entire United States entered the Great Depression, the worst economic downturn in the country's history. Banks failed, businesses closed, and people lost their jobs. Strikes were common. In September 1934, textile workers clashed with police, leaving three people dead. Governor Green finally called in the National Guard to end the strike. By 1937, many of the state's textile mills had closed for good.

In 1932, Americans elected Franklin D. Roosevelt president. The next year, he began the New Deal, a series of programs to help residents hurt by the Depression. One program, the Civilian Conservation Corps, hired young Rhode Islanders

## POLITICAL LEADER

In 1920, women across the United States won the right to vote. Two years later, Isabelle Ahearn O'Neill (1880–1975) became the first woman to serve in the Rhode Island General Assembly. O'Neill, the daughter of Irish immigrants, was born in Woonsocket. Before entering politics, she had acted in several silent films and taught in Providence. During part of her eight years in the Rhode Island House of Representatives, she served as a Democratic Party leader. She went on to serve two years in the state senate. In 1933, President Franklin D. Roosevelt named her to a U.S. agency that fought illegal drug use. O'Neill is remembered today as a pioneering female politician.

## WORD TO KNOW

**federal** *relating to the national government*

### Q8 WHAT IS A QUONSET HUT?

**A8** A Quonset hut is a portable building with a distinctive half-cylinder shape and was designed at Quonset Point Naval Air Station in 1941. The huts were used to house soldiers and equipment throughout World War II. Eight people could set up one of the 48-foot-long (15 m) steel huts in one day.

Quonset hut

to work on projects such as building trails and roads. The Social Security system, which gives money to retired workers and people who cannot work, was also started during this time.

Even with help from the **federal** government, Rhode Islanders struggled to survive. As Native Americans and English colonists had done hundreds of years before, some Rhode Islanders went to the shore and caught lobsters or dug for shellfish to feed their families.

## WORLD WAR II

The New Deal provided some relief, but it did not end the Great Depression. Instead, the Depression ended when World War II began. Millions of Americans found jobs building airplanes, weapons, and other military supplies.

The war began in Europe in September 1939. The United States entered in December 1941, after Japan launched a surprise attack on the U.S. naval base at Pearl Harbor, Hawai'i. Rhode Islanders did their part in the war effort. More than 92,000 men and women served in the military.

Those who did not join the military also did their part. At the Walsh-Kaiser shipyard in Providence, workers turned out 63 ships for the U.S. Navy. The workers included 3,000 women. Millions of women across the country worked in defense plants during the war, filling the places of men who had joined the armed forces.

Rhode Island was the site of three navy bases: a naval air station at Quonset Point, the Davisville Naval Base, and the U.S. Naval Training Station in Newport. At Davisville, the first Seabees trained for action. The Seabees were soldiers who were also trained as engineers. They built roads, airstrips, and buildings on the Pacific islands that the United States won from Japan during the war. The soldiers' nickname came from the first letters of their official military unit name: *Construction Battalion*.

## POSTWAR CHANGES

The war ended in 1945, and the soldiers came home. To help veterans restart their lives, Congress had passed the GI Bill, which provided them with money for college and cheap loans to buy homes.

In the years after the war, many young families in Rhode Island and elsewhere left the cities for the suburbs. Less well-off residents tended to remain in Providence, where housing was cheaper. But crime began to be a problem. In 1950, Providence was home to nearly 250,000 people, but 20 years later its population had fallen to 179,000. Many of the people went to nearby Warwick and Cranston, where families found bigger yards, better schools, and less crime.

The postwar years saw the first interstate highways crisscross Rhode Island. They made it easier for people to work in the city and drive home to the suburbs at night. As new shopping centers and malls opened in the suburbs, many Providence department stores closed their doors. The new highways also greatly reduced travel times to Boston, Massachusetts. Many Rhode Islanders began traveling to Boston to work at higher-paying jobs.

The state's economy suffered throughout this period. Many factories moved out of state or closed their doors entirely. For a time, the U.S. Navy provided jobs, but in 1973, the navy moved part of its fleet out of Newport, putting 16,000 people out of work. In the decades after World War II, Rhode Islanders faced higher unemployment and lower wages than workers in many parts of the country. Many businesses avoided Rhode Island because the state had higher taxes than other states, and lawmakers were thought to favor workers over businesses.

Meanwhile, corruption plagued Rhode Island politics during the 1980s and 1990s. Several government officials, including Providence mayor Buddy Cianci, a state supreme court judge, and Governor Edward D. DiPrete, were convicted of crimes.

## RHODE ISLAND TODAY

Rhode Islanders are optimistic about their state. Since the 1970s, state, federal, and private money have been used to reinvigorate cities such as Providence and Newport. In the 1990s, Providence had a rebirth, during which the city built parks and river walks along its waterfront. In Newport, 18th- and 19th-century mansions were renovated and today serve as museums in the city's bustling tourist industry.

Rhode Islanders faced tough times in March 2010 when record rainfall caused many rivers and streams to overflow. The water flooded roads, homes, and businesses around the state. Thousands of Rhode Islanders were left without power, and thousands more were evacuated from their homes. The federal government pledged millions of dollars to help Rhode Islanders recover and rebuild.

Today, Rhode Island continues to be a magnet for immigrants, particularly from Spanish-speaking and Asian countries. The state's Hispanic population grew from 4.6 percent of Rhode Islanders in 1990 to 12.5 percent in 2010. The Asian population grew from 1.8 percent to 3.0 percent of Rhode Islanders during the same time. Many immigrants settle in and around Providence. These days, people of many different backgrounds believe their little state has a big future.

## SEE IT HERE!

### WATERFIRE

Artist Barnaby Evans created a sculpture titled *WaterFire* in Providence in 1994. The sculpture consists of 100 metal baskets sitting on posts in the rivers that had been uncovered. Several nights a year, the baskets are filled with wood logs that are set ablaze. The flames, their reflections, and the city skyline create a striking sight. Music plays along the riverbanks as the fires burn through the night. *WaterFire* has drawn visitors from around the world and is among the brightest signs of Providence's continuing importance to Rhode Island.

*WaterFire* along the Providence River

## READ ABOUT

Diners enjoy a meal
on Bannister's
Wharf in Newport.

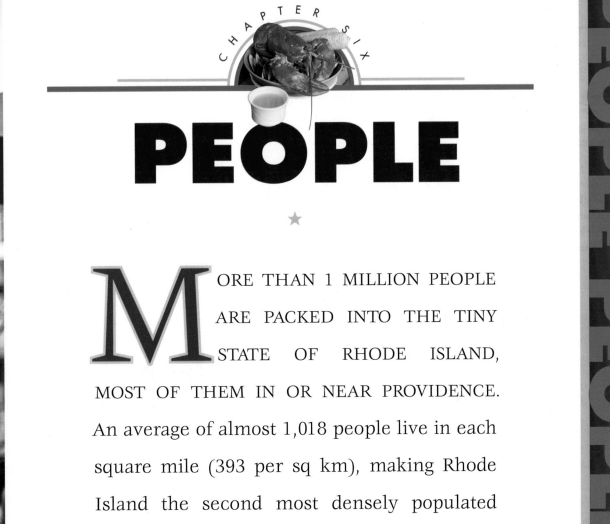

# CHAPTER SIX

# PEOPLE

★

MORE THAN 1 MILLION PEOPLE ARE PACKED INTO THE TINY STATE OF RHODE ISLAND, MOST OF THEM IN OR NEAR PROVIDENCE. An average of almost 1,018 people live in each square mile (393 per sq km), making Rhode Island the second most densely populated state in the country after New Jersey. But most Rhode Islanders don't mind. One advantage of living in a small state is that no matter where you are, pockets of quiet countryside or wide sandy beaches are never too far away.

## Big City Life

This list shows the population of Rhode Island's biggest cities

Providence . . . . . . . .178,042
Warwick . . . . . . . . . . 82,672
Cranston . . . . . . . . . .80,387
Pawtucket . . . . . . . . .71,148
East Providence . . . . . .47,037

Source: U.S. Census Bureau, 2010 census

## AT HOME IN RHODE ISLAND

Providence is the largest city in Rhode Island. The four next-largest cities are near Providence. The state's smallest towns lie along the border with Connecticut and the southern shore. Even these areas, though, are close enough to cities to be called urban areas.

## WHO'S A RHODE ISLANDER?

Over the centuries, people from all over the world have settled in Rhode Island. Today's residents trace their roots to dozens of countries. Topping the list is Ireland, fol-

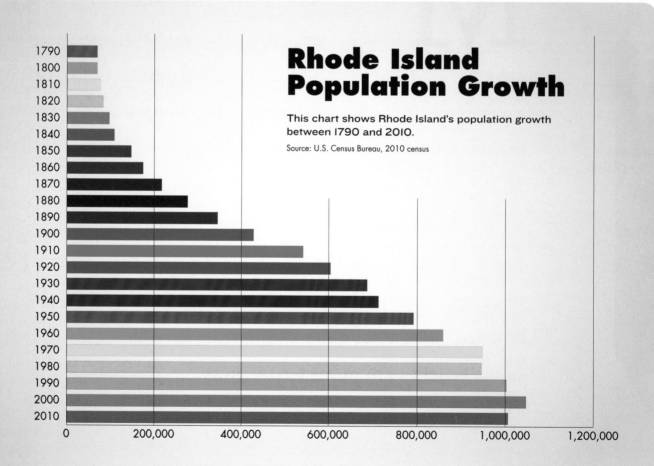

# Rhode Island Population Growth

This chart shows Rhode Island's population growth between 1790 and 2010.

Source: U.S. Census Bureau, 2010 census

A traditional Laotian wedding ceremony in Providence

lowed closely by Italy. Many Rhode Islanders also trace their roots to England, French Canada, and Portugal. English settlers helped turn Rhode Island from a colony to a state, while French Canadians worked in the mills. Nearly 10 percent of Rhode Islanders are of Portuguese descent—the highest percentage of any state in the country. Many Portuguese have worked as fishers along the state's shores.

People of African descent have lived in Rhode Island since the 1600s. Today, African Americans make up about 5 percent of the state's population. Most black Rhode Islanders live in Providence and other cities.

People from Spanish-speaking countries are Rhode Island's largest immigrant group today. Hispanics began arriving in large numbers during the 1970s. The first to arrive were Puerto Ricans and Colombians; more recently, many Mexicans, Dominicans, and Guatemalans have arrived. The Hispanic population grew by nearly 30,000 people between 2000 and 2010. Many of these newcomers settled in Providence neighborhoods that had welcomed earlier generations of immigrants from Europe.

Asians have also come to Rhode Island, primarily from Vietnam, Cambodia, and China. Most settled near Providence.

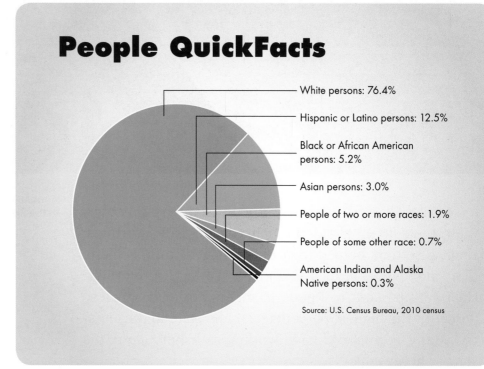

## People QuickFacts

White persons: 76.4%

Hispanic or Latino persons: 12.5%

Black or African American persons: 5.2%

Asian persons: 3.0%

People of two or more races: 1.9%

People of some other race: 0.7%

American Indian and Alaska Native persons: 0.3%

Source: U.S. Census Bureau, 2010 census

# Where Rhode Islanders Live

The colors on this map indicate population density throughout the state. The darker the color, the more people live there.

People per square mile

- 10,000 or more
- 5,000 to 10,000
- 1,000 to 5,000
- 500 to 1,000
- 200 to 500
- 100 to 200
- 100 or fewer

MASSACHUSETTS

Woonsocket

Pascoag

Chepachet

Blackstone

Valley Falls

Smithfield

Central Falls

Pawtucket

North Providence

Scituate

Providence

MASSACHUSETTS

Cranston

East Providence

Scituate Reservoir

Barrington

Warren

West Warwick

Warwick

Bristol

East Greenwich

Providence

Narragansett Bay

Sakonnet

Tiverton

Portsmouth

North Kingstown

Wood

Jamestown

Middletown

Little Compton

West Kingston

Bridgetown

Pawcatuck

Kingston

Newport

South Kingstown

Charlestown

Rhode Island Sound

CONNECTICUT

Westerly

Block Island Sound

ATLANTIC OCEAN

N W E S

NEW YORK

Block Island

New Shoreham

0        10 Miles

0        10 Kilometers

Religion has always played a large part in Rhode Island life. In colonial days, Baptist, Quaker, and Jewish people found a home there, when the Puritan colonies surrounding Rhode Island were not welcoming. Starting in the 19th century, most of the immigrants to the state came from Roman Catholic lands, and today Rhode Island is the nation's most heavily Catholic state. Forty-six percent of Rhode Islanders are Catholic.

**Harlan Huckleby invented the "bubbler" water fountain in 1889. Unlike other fountains of its time, Huckleby's invention shot a stream of water into the air so people could sip it up.**

## HOW TO TALK LIKE A RHODE ISLANDER

Traveling across Rhode Island, you're bound to hear some words or expressions that leave you a little confused. If you're dying for a drink, a Rhode Islander might direct you to a bubbler—the state's word for a water fountain. And Rhode Islanders love to drink coffee-flavored milk shakes, which they call coffee cabinets. Want a long, meat-stuffed sandwich to go with that? Ask for a grinder, which in other parts of the United States is a sub, a hero, or a hoagie. Would you rather have a hot dog? Then go to a weiner place. If all these things are on sale, Rhode Islanders say they're on special.

## HOW TO EAT LIKE A RHODE ISLANDER

For centuries, Rhode Islanders have looked to the sea and Narragansett Bay for some of their favorite foods. That love of fish and shellfish continues today. Many Rhode Islanders enjoy clambakes, which feature clams, lobster, corn, and potatoes all cooked together, either on a stove or outdoors over hot rocks, wood coals, and seaweed. The first clambakes took place long before the English came to Rhode Island, when Algonquian Indians roasted clams, oysters, and lobsters over hot stones.

Italian immigrants brought their love of food to Rhode Island, and pizzerias and Italian restaurants are found all over the state. A *wandi*— deep-fried pastry—is a common treat. These sweet treats are sometimes called doughboys.

Lobster, clams, corn, and melted butter at a clambake

# MENU

## WHAT'S ON THE MENU IN RHODE ISLAND?

### Rhode Island Clam Chowder

All clam chowders feature bits of clams, potatoes, and vegetables in a broth, but only Rhode Islanders serve it in a clear broth. Typical Rhode Island chowder uses quahogs.

### Stuffies

A stuffy is a baked quahog clam stuffed with bread crumbs, herbs, and sometimes bacon or a sausage called chorizo.

### Coffee Syrup

Rhode Island is the coffee syrup capital of the United States, since it's home to the only company that makes it. This sweet, coffee-flavored liquid is added to milk to make the official state drink—coffee milk. The syrup is also a key ingredient in a coffee cabinet.

### Frozen Lemonade

Need to cool off on a hot day? Then try one of Rhode Island's favorite summertime treats: frozen lemonade. Shavings of ice are mixed with bits of fresh lemons and sugar.

### Dynamite

The small northern town of Woonsocket is home to one explosive sandwich—the dynamite. Hamburger, peppers, onions, and tomato sauce are mixed together to create a sloppy, spicy filling for long rolls.

Frozen lemonade

### TRY THIS RECIPE
### Johnnycakes

When is a pancake not a pancake? When it's made in Rhode Island and called a johnnycake. These Rhode Island specialties are made with cornmeal rather than flour. Have an adult nearby when you make this recipe.

**Ingredients:**

1 cup cornmeal
½ teaspoon salt
2 teaspoons sugar (optional)
1 to 1½ cups boiling water
3 tablespoons milk
3 tablespoons vegetable oil (or bacon fat)

**Instructions:**

1. Mix together all the dry ingredients in a bowl.
2. Use a whisk to stir in the boiling water until the mixture is mushy.
3. Whisk in the milk until the batter is smooth.
4. Heat a heavy frying pan over medium-high heat and add the oil or fat.
5. Spoon out enough of the mixture onto the pan to make a cake about ¼ inch thick and 3 inches wide.
6. Cook each side for about 4 to 5 minutes, until brown.
7. Serve the johnnycakes with maple syrup and butter.

Stuffies

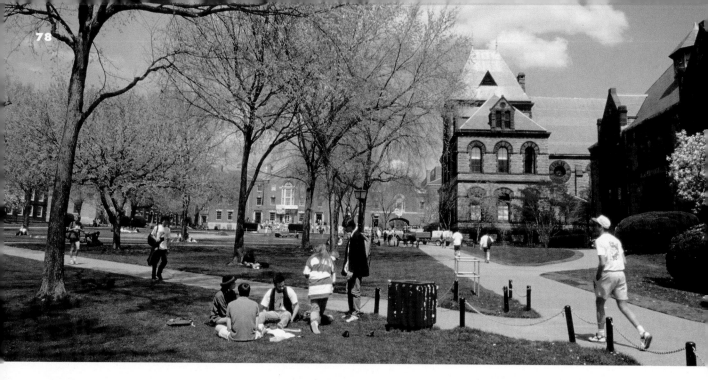

**Students on the Brown University campus**

# EDUCATION

When the morning school bell rings, some 142,000 Rhode Island students head out to the state's public schools. Other students attend private schools, some of which are run by religious organizations. Still others enroll in charter schools, which are special public schools that are free from many local rules. They receive money from the state and take donations. Charter schools sometimes focus on a particular area of study, such as math or science.

After high school, students from all over the globe head to Rhode Island's colleges and universities. The oldest is Brown University in Providence, which belongs to the Ivy League, a group of some of the most prestigious private colleges in the country. Ruth J. Simmons became the first African American president of an Ivy League school when she was sworn in as president of Brown University in 2001.

Also located in Providence is the Rhode Island School of Design (RISD), one of the country's best art schools. There is also Johnson and Wales University, which has an outstanding culinary, or cooking, program. Another private school, Roger Williams University, includes Rhode Island's only law school.

Public state universities include the United States Naval War College in Newport, where naval officers are trained. The main campus of the University of Rhode Island, the state's largest public school, is in Kingston. Other public institutions include the Community College of Rhode Island and Rhode Island College.

## TALENTS OF ALL KINDS

Since colonial days, Rhode Islanders have shown great skill in producing beautiful things. In the 18th century, John Goddard and John Townsend created attractive, practical wooden furniture. Crafting items out of silver takes tremendous skill, and Jabez Gorham was one of the best. In 1813, he began working in Providence and built a successful business. His company made the statue named *Independent Man*, which tops Rhode Island's capitol.

In 1989, a desk made by John Goddard sold for $12.1 million! It set the record for the highest price for a piece of furniture made in the United States.

A desk from John Townsend's shop, 1800s

*Independent Man*, on top of the state capitol

## EDWARD BANNISTER: PRIZE-WINNING PAINTER

Edward Bannister (1828–1901) was born in Canada and learned how to paint after settling in Boston. He moved to Providence in 1870, and most of his best work was done there. He was one of the first commercially successful African American painters. His 1876 work *Under the Oaks* won first prize at the Philadelphia Centennial Exhibition. Another painting from that year, *Oak Trees*, is featured above. Today, his work is on display at museums around the country.

**Want to know more?** Visit www.factsfor now.scholastic.com and enter the keywords **Rhode Island**.

After the American Revolution, Gilbert Stuart of North Kingstown was one of the country's foremost painters. His portrait of President George Washington is on the dollar bill. In the late 1800s, Edward Bannister created paintings of idealized landscapes.

## A WAY WITH WORDS

Some of Rhode Island's earliest leaders were notable writers, including Roger Williams. He wrote several books on religious issues and published a book on the Narragansett people and their language, *A Key into the Language of America*. The 19th-century poet Julia Ward Howe, who wrote the lyrics to "Battle Hymn of the Republic," was related to two colonial governors of

Rick Benjamin was named Rhode Island's state poet in 2012.

Rhode Island. More recently, Rick Benjamin, who teaches at Brown University, has written poems with a strong Rhode Island voice. In 2012, he was named the state poet.

Children's author Avi spent many years living in Providence and set some of his books there, including *Something Upstairs: A Tale of Ghosts*. In 2003, he won the Newbery Medal—given to the best children's book of the year—for *Crispin: The Cross of Lead*. Natalie Babbitt, an award-winning children's author who lives in Providence, wrote the fantasy book *Tuck Everlasting*. Another Rhode Island author who kids—and adults—enjoying reading is David Macaulay. After studying architecture at RISD, he went on to write and illustrate books such as *The Way Things Work* and *Pyramid*.

**MINI-BIO**

## JULIA WARD HOWE: POET OF THE REPUBLIC

Julia Ward Howe (1819–1910) devoted her life to words and helping others. She published her first work while still a teen, and she went on to write poems, plays, and essays. Howe strongly opposed slavery and called for giving women the right to vote. In 1861, while the Civil War raged, she wrote the lyrics for the song "The Battle Hymn of the Republic." She set the words to an existing tune called "John Brown's Body." The song was meant to inspire Union troops fighting against the South. The lyrics remain her best-known work.

**?** **Want to know more?** Visit www.factsfor now.scholastic.com and enter the keywords **Rhode Island**.

## STAGE AND SCREEN

One of the greatest entertainers of the early 20th century hailed from Rhode Island. George M. Cohan was born in Providence to a family of traveling entertainers who soon put young George in their act. He became a singer, dancer, and producer. He also wrote songs such as "I'm a Yankee Doodle Dandy" and "Give My Regards to Broadway."

Rhode Islanders have perhaps made their biggest screen impact behind the camera. Michael Corrente of Pawtucket has directed several films that were also shot in

## SISSIERETTA JOYNER JONES: SINGER SUPREME

Sissieretta Joyner Jones (1869–1933) was born in Virginia and moved to Providence as a child, where she soon impressed members of her church with her singing talents. She studied music and began her professional career in 1888. Her extraordinary voice won her many admirers, and she gave private concerts for several U.S. presidents. But as an African American, she was not allowed to sing in the world's great opera houses, despite her talents. In 1915, she returned to Rhode Island to take care of her sick mother and never sang professionally again.

**? Want to know more?** Visit www.factsfor now.scholastic.com and enter the keywords **Rhode Island**.

Providence, such as *Outside Providence*. For television, Seth MacFarlane created *Family Guy*, which features Peter Griffin and his wacky family. MacFarlane, who went to RISD, set the show in the made-up town of Quahog, Rhode Island.

Movies and TV shows rely on music to add to their emotional impact. Two Rhode Islanders made their careers writing music for films. Pawtucket's Wendy Carlos wrote the music for *Tron* and other movies. She was the first musician to introduce the synthesizer, a computerized keyboard, to a wide audience. Bill Conti of Providence wrote the music for most of the *Rocky* films and a number of popular TV shows.

Some Rhode Island singers have found success onstage. Opera singer Sissieretta Joyner Jones was the first African American to perform at New York's Carnegie Hall.

## THE LONGEST GAME

Pawtucket's McCoy Stadium was the site of the longest professional baseball game ever played. The game—between the Pawtucket Red Sox and the Rochester (New York) Red Wings—began at 8:00 P.M. on April 18, 1981. At 4:09 A.M. the next morning, the game was stopped with the score tied after 32 innings. The final inning was played about two months later, with the PawSox winning 3–2.

## SPORTS

Rhode Island doesn't have any major league sports teams. Most sports fans follow the pro teams in nearby Boston, while also rooting for minor league teams such as the Pawtucket Red Sox (baseball) and the Providence Bruins (hockey).

College teams attract lots of fans. The Providence College Friars have fielded many good teams in men's basketball, and the University of Rhode Island Rams were once a basketball powerhouse. The fast break—when a player rebounds an opponent's missed shot and then quickly moves to the other end of the court to take a shot—was supposedly perfected at the University of Rhode Island under Hall of Fame coach Frank Keaney.

Rhode Island has also produced great athletes. Hall of Fame baseball player Napoleon "Nap" Lajoie was one of the greatest hitters of the early 20th century. And Ellison Myers Brown was a two-time winner of the Boston Marathon, one of the world's premier long-distance races.

In the past, Newport was a leader in American sports. The first polo match on U.S. soil took place there in 1876, as did the first open golf tournament (1895) and the National Lawn Tennis Championship (1881). Newport is also the home of the International Tennis Hall of Fame, and the city has hosted many America's Cup races, the top sailing event in the world.

## MINI-BIO

### ELLISON MYERS BROWN: MARATHON MAN

Ellison Myers Brown (1913–1975) was a Narragansett from Westerly. His Narragansett name was Deerfoot, but running fans knew him as Tarzan. He ran marathons, 26-mile (42 km) road races that push runners to the limit. He raced in the Boston Marathon nine times, winning twice. In 1936, he represented the United States at the Berlin Olympics. Brown was known for his great speed and endurance.

**?** **Want to know more?** Visit www.factsfor now.scholastic.com and enter the keywords **Rhode Island**.

A match at the International Tennis Hall of Fame in Newport

# READ ABOUT

Governor Lincoln
Chafee prepares to
sign Rhode Island's
Marriage Equality
Act into law in 2013.

CHAPTER SEVEN

# GOVERNMENT

★

EACH YEAR, RHODE ISLAND HIGH SCHOOL STUDENTS TAKE PART IN THE CAPITOL FORUM. The students meet at the Rhode Island State House and discuss key international issues. Then they vote on the ones that concern them most. Their views are then sent to U.S. lawmakers in Washington, D.C. In 2011, Rhode Island students discussed the role of the United States in the global economy, the use of American military force in foreign conflicts, and the environment. Fifty-five students and 15 teachers participated in the forum that year.

Rhode Island once had five state capitals—at the same time! It had one for each county.

## THE CENTER OF THE GOVERNMENT

Providence is the capital of Rhode Island, and most major government officials have their offices there or in neighboring towns. The most impressive state building in the capital is the State House, which sits on Smith Hill. On its three floors, elected officials shape the state's laws. Both the legislature and the office of the governor are in the State House.

The details of Rhode Island's government are spelled out in the state constitution. The first one came into effect in 1843, and many amendments have been made over the years.

# Capital City

This map shows places of interest in Providence, Rhode Island's capital city.

The state capitol in Providence

Rhode Island's government, like the federal government, has three branches. The legislative branch makes laws. The executive branch carries out the laws and sometimes proposes new ones. The judicial branch makes sure the laws are carried out fairly.

## THE EXECUTIVE BRANCH

The governor is the head of the executive branch. He or she either accepts or rejects proposed laws, called bills,

# Capitol Facts

Here are some fascinating facts about Rhode Island's state capitol.

**Size**. . . . . . . . . . . . . . . . . . . . . . . 330 feet (101 m) long, 180 feet (55 m) wide, 233 feet (71 m) high
**Year completed**. . . . . . . . . . . . . . . . . . . . . . . . . . . . . . . . . . . . . . . . . . . . . . . 1900
**Dome**. . . . . . . . . . . . . . . . . . . . . . . . . . . . . . Fourth-largest self-supporting dome in the world
**Statue on top**. . . . . . . .*Independent Man* stands 11 feet (3.4 m) tall and weighs about 500 pounds (227 kg)

# Rhode Island State Government

**EXECUTIVE BRANCH**
Carries out state laws

Governor

Lieutenant Governor

Secretary of State

General Treasurer

Attorney General

Department heads of:
Agriculture
Education
Corrections
Revenue
and many more

**JUDICIAL BRANCH**
Enforces state laws

Supreme Court

Superior Court

Family Court

Workers Compensation Court

Traffic Tribunal

**LEGISLATIVE BRANCH**
Makes and passes state laws

General Assembly
(2 divisions)

Senate
(38 members)

House of Representatives
(75 members)

that have been passed by the legislature. The governor can issue executive orders, which do not have to be approved by lawmakers. The governor is also responsible for proposing a state budget, but state lawmakers have the final say on how much money is spent. The governor also chooses people to lead various departments. The state senate must approve most of these choices.

Rhode Islanders also elect a lieutenant governor, who takes over if the governor can no longer serve. Day to day, the lieutenant governor works on important state issues, such as providing affordable health care and supporting small businesses.

Other executive branch officials include the secretary of state, who is in charge of running elections. The general treasurer invests the state's money, looking for the safest ways to make more of it. The attorney general makes sure the state's laws are enforced and represents Rhode Island in legal matters. In 2006, Rhode Island attorney general Patrick Lynch won the first lawsuit in the nation against companies that made lead paint, which can cause severe illnesses. As a result, the companies may have to pay up to $3.75 billion to remove the paint.

## THE LEGISLATIVE BRANCH

Rhode Island's lawmakers form the General Assembly, which includes the house of representatives and the senate. The representatives and senators propose, debate, change, and vote on bills. After both the house and the senate approve a bill, it is sent to the governor. Most bills

## SEE IT HERE!

### OLD STATE HOUSE

The current Rhode Island State House replaced one that opened in 1762. That older building is known as the Old State House. Several historic events took place in the Old State House. On May 4, 1776, Rhode Island lawmakers broke their allegiance to Great Britain's King George III. After the American Revolution, state lawmakers met there and called for the gradual freeing of Rhode Island's slaves. Today, the building is the home of the Rhode Island Historical Preservation & Heritage Commission.

### MINI-BIO

## ELIZABETH ROBERTS: DEDICATED PUBLIC SERVANT

Elizabeth Roberts (1957—) first ventured to Rhode Island from her native Virginia to attend Brown University. After school, she remained in the state to work and raise a family. In 1996, she was elected to the Rhode Island Senate, and she made health care one of her major issues. Though Roberts is a Democrat, her dedication earned her the respect of Republicans. In 2006, she was elected Rhode Island's first female lieutenant governor, and she was reelected in 2011. Roberts is leading the fight for affordable health care for all Rhode Islanders.

**?** **Want to know more?** Visit www.factsfornow .scholastic.com and enter the keywords **Rhode Island**.

The state house of representatives in session

can be passed in the General Assembly with a simple majority—half of the members present plus one. But any bill that deals with spending money for local or private purposes requires a three-fifths vote.

The legislature deals with issues ranging from the state budget to environmental protection. In 2013, the legislature passed a bill that established the state's minimum wage at $8.00 per hour, beginning January 1, 2014.

## THE JUDICIAL BRANCH

The judicial branch in Rhode Island has several layers. Judges are appointed by the governor, who chooses from a list proposed by a special judicial commission. The governor's selections

# Representing Rhode Island

This list shows the number of elected officials who represent Rhode Island, both on the state and national levels.

| OFFICE | NUMBER | LENGTH OF TERM |
|---|---|---|
| State senators | 38 | 2 years |
| State representatives | 75 | 2 years |
| U.S. senators | 2 | 6 years |
| U.S. representatives | 2 | 2 years |
| Presidential electors | 4 | — |

must then be approved by the senate. The house must also approve candidates for the state supreme court. Once approved, Rhode Island judges serve for life.

The district court hears minor criminal cases and civil suits—suits between individuals or companies. More serious cases go to the superior court, which also hears **appeals** from the district court. The most powerful court in Rhode Island is the supreme court. It has five judges, called justices. The supreme court hears cases from the lower courts and also can decide if laws follow the state constitution.

The lower courts in Rhode Island include three that deal with specific legal issues. The workers compensation court settles disputes between employers and workers who claim they were injured on the job. The traffic tribunal hears most cases relating to traffic violations. The family court seeks to protect the health and safety of children.

## GOVERNMENT CLOSER TO HOME

Since colonial days, Rhode Island has had a tradition of strong local government. Each of the state's 39 towns and cities cherishes its independence, even as the state government has grown stronger over the years. Although Rhode Island is divided into five counties, it has no county government. Instead, towns make the final decisions on things such as local taxes, schooling, and building codes.

In Providence and other cities, a mayor, who serves as the executive, leads the government. An elected council forms the legislature, though the mayors have broad power to appoint members of city boards and commissions. Smaller towns usually have an elected council that hires a town manager to oversee the town's day-to-day operations. Some small towns also have town meetings, an old

## OFFERING A HELPING HAND

In 1973, U.S. senator Claiborne Pell called for a law to give money to college students who come from disadvantaged families. These funds became known as Pell Grants, and they are still given today. Pell served in the U.S. Senate from 1961 to 1997, longer than any other Rhode Islander.

### WORD TO KNOW

**appeals** *legal proceedings in which a court is asked to change the decision of a lower court*

# Rhode Island Counties

This map shows the five counties in Rhode Island. Providence, the state capital, is indicated with a star.

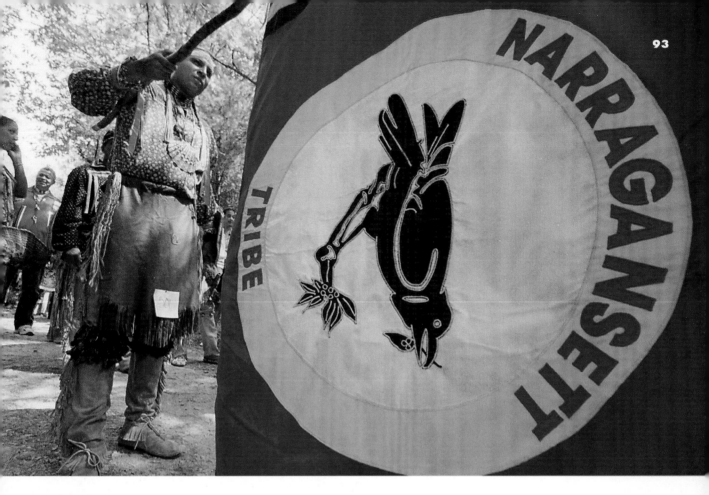

Members of the Narragansett Nation prepare for their annual meeting in Charlestown.

New England tradition. All town residents who attend the meeting can vote on how local taxes are spent and other important issues.

On the Narragansett lands in Charlestown, tribal members choose a chief sachem and a tribal council. These officials make business decisions for the tribes and provide essential services. Although Wampanoags and other Native Americans live in Rhode Island, the nation of Narragansetts is the only one recognized by the U.S. government. By U.S. law, each recognized tribe in the country is considered an independent nation, though its members are still U.S. citizens.

# State Flag

In 1897, Rhode Island became the third state to adopt an official state flag. The flag has a white background, with a golden anchor in the center. Underneath, a blue ribbon is inscribed with the word *Hope* in gold letters. Thirteen gold stars representing the original 13 states form a circle around the anchor and the ribbon.

# State Seal

Rhode Island's state seal shows a golden anchor with the word *Hope* above it. A border around the anchor reads "Seal of the State of Rhode Island and Providence Plantations 1636."

# READ ABOUT

Chemists at work in a laboratory in North Kingstown

# CHAPTER EIGHT

# ECONOMY

★

R HODE ISLAND IS SOMETIMES CALLED THE BIRTHPLACE OF THE AMERICAN INDUSTRIAL REVOLUTION, THANKS TO SAMUEL SLATER AND HIS COTTON MILL. Today, Rhode Island workers make a variety of products from jewelry to medicines to sleek yachts. Even more state residents make their living helping others— keeping them well, taking care of their money, running their governments. And state leaders hope to make Rhode Island a thriving home of new technology, to attract more workers and businesses to the state.

## FROM THE LAND AND SEA

Raising crops and livestock was once an important part of the Rhode Island economy. Breeders created two animals closely associated with the state. The Rhode Island Red chicken is the state bird, and the Narragansett pacer was once the most popular racing horse in North America. But today, farming and livestock make up just a small part of the economy, and Rhode Island ranks near the bottom of

# What Do Rhode Islanders Do?

This color-coded chart shows what industries Rhode Islanders work in.

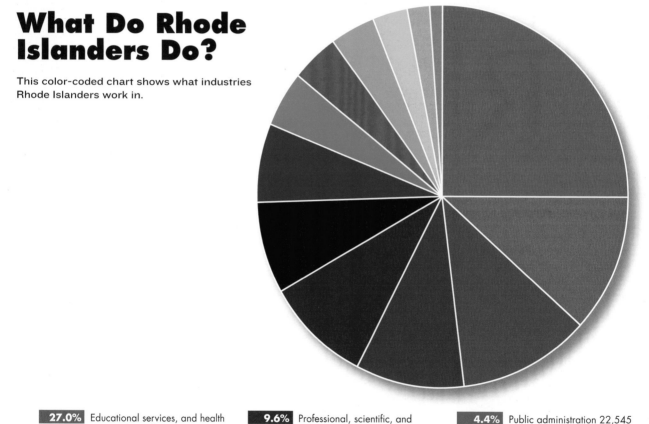

**27.0%** Educational services, and health care and social assistance 137,992

**11.9%** Retail trade 60,826

**11.6%** Manufacturing 59,190

**10.3%** Arts, entertainment, and recreation, and accommodation and food services 52,763

**9.6%** Professional, scientific, and management, and administrative and waste management services 49,049

**7.3%** Finance and insurance, and real estate and rental and leasing 37,530

**5.2%** Construction 26,513

**4.5%** Other services, except public administration 22,993

**4.4%** Public administration 22,545

**3.7%** Transportation and warehousing, and utilities 19,151

**2.3%** Wholesale trade 11,637

**1.8%** Information 8,969

**0.4%** Agriculture, forestry, fishing and hunting, and mining 2,165

Source: U.S. Census Bureau, 2010 census

Rhode Island fishers haul a net into their boat.

the 50 states in the value of its crops and livestock. Most farms and orchards are in the western part of the state. The top products are plants, trees, and flowers grown by nurseries and greenhouses, followed by corn and dairy products.

Fishing is another industry that was once key for Rhode Islanders but has gone into decline. Still, some fishing fleets leave the docks of towns such as Little Compton and Galilee, and clams and oysters are farmed in saltwater ponds and near Block Island. Recreational fishers, many of them tourists, add to Rhode Island's economy. They rent or buy equipment and spend money at restaurants and hotels.

## Top Products

| | |
|---|---|
| **Agriculture** | Greenhouse and nursery products, sweet corn, dairy products, potatoes, cattle, chickens, apples, hay, honey |
| **Manufacturing** | Electrical equipment, jewelry, silverware, computer and electronics products |
| **Mining** | Stone, sand, gravel |

# Major Agricultural and Mining Products

This map shows where Rhode Island's major agricultural and mining products come from. See a milk carton? That means dairy is found there.

Urban area

Farming

Forests, some farming

Cattle

Dairy

Fish

Fruit

Grains

Hay

Manufacturing

Mineral mining

Nursery products

Potatoes

Poultry

Shellfish

Vegetables

MASSACHUSETTS

Woonsocket

Chepachet

Pawtucket

Providence

CONNECTICUT

Cranston

MASSACHUSETTS

Warren

Warwick

Bristol

Tiverton

Portsmouth

Newport

Pawcatuck

Charlestown

Westerly

Rhode Island Sound

ATLANTIC OCEAN

Block Island Sound

Block Island

0    10 Miles
0    10 Kilometers

**WOW**

Rhode Island mining operations account for about $43 million worth of minerals, metals, and fuel products each year. The state's 30 mining companies directly employ nearly 500 people, with another 2,800 people working in related mining activities.

## MAKING GOODS

Manufacturing is in decline across New England, including in Rhode Island. Many mills and factories have been torn down or turned into offices, housing, or stores. Manufacturing jobs in Rhode Island decreased from 50,800 in 2007 to 40,300 in 2013. However, Rhode Island is still a world leader in producing inexpensive jewelry, and some textiles continue to be made in the state. Rhode Island's top manufactured products are all kinds of electrical equipment and parts. Electric Boat, a company in Quonset Point, builds submarines for the U.S. Navy.

Some Rhode Island manufacturers are devoted to making life more fun. The state is home to several yacht and sailboat builders, including LaserPerformance Sailboats in Portsmouth and Goetz Boats in St. Bristol. And the headquarters for Hasbro, the creator of Monopoly and Fisher-Price toys, is in Pawtucket.

High-tech industries have been growing in Rhode Island. Companies such as Tellart, in Providence, design new ways to use computers. APC by Schneider Electric, in West Kingston, is part of a company that sells more than $3.5 billion worth of backup power sources for computers.

### HENRY HASSENFELD: TOY MAN

A Jewish immigrant from Poland, Henry Hassenfeld (?–1960) began his business empire in 1923, selling textile scraps. With his brother Helal, he founded Hassenfeld Brothers. The company, which later became Hasbro, soon began making school supplies and, finally, toys. Henry and his sons Merrill and Harold were running the company when they introduced the first toy ever advertised on television: Mr. Potato Head. Hasbro became one of the largest toy companies in the world. Some of its popular products are Transformers, G.I. Joe, and Monopoly. Henry Hassenfeld's family still plays a role in running the company.

**?** **Want to know more?** Visit www.factsfornow.scholastic.com and enter the keywords **Rhode Island**.

## SEE IT HERE!

### MR. POTATO HEAD

As the home of toy company Hasbro, Rhode Island has proudly called itself the "Birthplace of Fun." How better to show this than through one of the company's most beloved creations? In 2000, Mr. Potato Head was named Rhode Island's family travel ambassador. Nearly 50 uniquely designed statues of the character were placed around the state. Some of these can still be seen, including the "original," located at Hasbro Headquarters in Pawtucket.

## MINI-BIO

### MATT COTTAM: DESIGN WIZARD

After graduating from the Rhode Island School of Design, Matt Cottam (1973—) stayed in Providence and cofounded his own design business. His company, Tellart, makes sensors that can detect heat, motion, sound, or light and then use that energy to control motors or send information to a Web site. He has also worked with Brown University students to design a new kind of suit worn by people who handle hazardous materials such as deadly chemicals. With the new suit, a person can get dressed alone, rather than needing help, as with the old suits. Cottam's suits also offer more protection. His design work highlights the new, creative thinking going on in Rhode Island industry.

**Want to know more?** Visit www.factsfornow.scholastic.com and enter the keywords **Rhode Island**.

Some companies in Rhode Island work in biotechnology, which uses **genetic engineering** to make products, such as medicines. In 2005, Amgen opened a plant in West Greenwich that makes medication for arthritis, a joint disease, and for high cholesterol, which can cause heart disease. Neurotech, in Cumberland, uses biotechnology to develop treatments for blindness. Scientists at Providence-based EpiVax use cutting-edge science to improve vaccines. State officials hope the state's biotechnology industry will continue to grow. A law passed in 2006 lowered taxes for companies that use genetic engineering to make products. This law encourages more biotechnology companies to come to Rhode Island.

### WORD TO KNOW

**genetic engineering** *changing genes, the chemicals in plants and animals that determine the traits passed from one generation to the next*

## SERVICES OF ALL KINDS

When you go to the bank, buy a burger, or take your bike in for repairs, you're using the services of a company. In Rhode Island, service industries dominate the economy. These industries help people invest their money, provide health care, teach children, and sell goods. Lifespan hospital group is the state's largest nongovernment employer, with nearly 12,000 service workers. Woonsocket is the home of one of the country's top drugstores, CVS Caremark. The company employs 5,800 Rhode Islanders.

Bakers and chefs are among the many service workers who contribute to Rhode Island's economy.

The state's media—newspapers, TV and radio stations, and Web sites—help keep Rhode Islanders informed about events in the state, across the country, and around the world. The state's largest newspaper is the *Providence Journal*. Several other cities, including Woonsocket and Pawtucket, also have daily papers. Rhode Island has five television stations. Many viewers also watch channels that are produced in neighboring Massachusetts.

Everyone loves a good vacation, and Rhode Islanders are no different. They, along with visitors from other states, spend almost $5.2 billion every year on tourism. Tourism is the state's fastest-growing industry. Tourists are attracted to the state's beaches, waters, and historic sites.

MASSACHUSETTS

Woonsocket

Blackstone

*Chepachet*

Chepachet

Smithfield

44

Central
Falls

Valley Falls

1

95

North Providence

**Providence**

Pawtucket

44

6

Scituate

295

MASSACHUSETTS

195

*Scituate
Reservoir*

Cranston

East Providence

West
Warwick

*Pawtuxet*

Barrington

Warren

Geographic Center
of Rhode Island

Warwick

*Providence*

Bristol

East Greenwich

*Narragansett Bay*

Portsmouth

Tiverton

95

Prudence Island

*Sakonnet*

CONNECTICUT

North Kingstown

Rhode
Island

Middletown

*Wood*

Jamestown

Little Compton

Kingston

*Pawcatuck*

1

Newport

Charlestown

Conanicut
Island

*Rhode Island Sound*

Westerly

N
W        E
S

*Block Island Sound*

*ATLANTIC
OCEAN*

Block
Island

New Shoreham

0          10 Miles

0          10 Kilometers

| | |
|---|---|
| 95 | Interstate highway |
| 1 | Other highway |

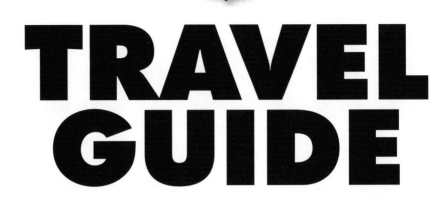

# TRAVEL GUIDE

★

DON'T LET ITS SMALL SIZE FOOL YOU—RHODE ISLAND IS CHOCK-FULL OF THINGS TO DO AND PLACES TO SEE. You can explore Newport's historic buildings, gaze at stunning art at the Rhode Island School of Design Museum, and head out onto Narragansett Bay for some of the best sailing in the country. So pack your bags, and let's take a big tour of the smallest state!

←—Follow along with this travel map. We'll begin in Providence and travel all the way to Charlestown.

## THE CAPITAL REGION

**THINGS TO DO:** Shop in America's oldest mall, see the country's first mill, and get a good look at an anteater.

### Providence

★ **First Baptist Church:** In 1638, Roger Williams started the first Baptist church in North America. By the 1770s, the members decided they needed a new home, and they built this grand church. The church features beautiful carved wood, a crystal chandelier, and a 185-foot-tall (56 m) steeple.

★ **Roger Williams Park Zoo:** This zoo is Rhode Island's top outdoor tourist attraction and one of the oldest zoos in the United States. It has elephants, giraffes, polar bears, anteaters, and many more creatures.

Polar bears at the Roger Williams Park Zoo

## SEE IT HERE!

### BIG BLUE BUG

Driving on Interstate 95 in Providence, it's hard to miss the Big Blue Bug. The steel, wire-mesh, and fiberglass termite weighs in at 2 tons and is 58 feet (18 m) long. The giant termite, which was named Nibbles Woodaway in a contest, was erected in 1980 to advertise a pest-control business. Since then, it has been featured in many movies and TV shows. Each Christmas, it's dressed up with a Santa beard.

Italian ice cream called gelato

★ **Federal Hill:** Getting hungry for some pasta, pizza, or creamy Italian ice cream? Then Federal Hill is the place to go. Almost 50 restaurants are packed into the neighborhood, which has been populated by Italian Americans for more than 100 years. In recent years, Mexican and Indian restaurants have added to the area's eating delights.

Visitors at the Rhode Island School of Design Museum

★ **Rhode Island School of Design Museum:** Stand beneath a towering but serene Asian statue, or immerse yourself in a painting of a misty landscape. Don't like those? Then keep moving, because there's a lot more to see at the school's art museum. Its collection includes more than 80,000 pieces.

★ **Rhode Island Black Heritage Society:** African Americans played a huge part in Rhode Island's history. This museum tells the story of the state's African Americans in colonial and modern times.

★ **The Arcade:** When the Arcade opened in 1828, it was the first indoor shopping mall in the United States. Shoppers still come to the Arcade for a bargain—and to see a little bit of history.

★ **American Diner Museum:** This museum contains company records, drawings, promotional brochures, and equipment from several diner manufacturing companies along with a few diner cars.

★ **Providence Children's Museum:** If you want to explore the whats and whys of water, this museum is the place for you. There are also exhibits on subjects ranging from the human body to the settlers of Rhode Island.

## East Providence

★ **Crescent Park Carousel:** Here the music still plays and the horses still whirl. Opened in 1895, the ride was designed by Charles I. D. Looff, a master carousel maker who immigrated from Denmark. His creation in East Providence has 66 hand-carved horses, and the tails are made from real horsehair!

Carousel pony at Crescent Park

### Pawtucket

★ **Slater Mill:** Samuel Slater opened the nation's first mechanized textile mill on this site in 1793. Today, that building and the waterwheel that powered his machines still stand. Another mill building from 1810 features working textile machines.

### Cranston

★ **Sprague Mansion:** Governor William Sprague came from one of America's wealthiest families, and his family's 28-room mansion was the site of large, fancy parties. Sprague eventually lost most of his fortune and had to sell the home. Today, ghosts of his father and several others are said to haunt the house. Visit it—if you dare!

# NORTHERN RHODE ISLAND

**THINGS TO DO:** Explore the Blackstone River, see the silliness at the Ancient and Horribles Parade, and have some quiet time outdoors at a nature refuge.

### Woonsocket

★ **Museum of Work and Culture:** This museum follows the journey of French Canadians who left their homes in Canada to work in the mills of Rhode Island.

★ **Blackstone River Rapids:** The Blackstone River cuts through northeastern Rhode Island, and its waters have powered many of the state's mills. Today, thrill seekers rush over its rapids in canoes and kayaks.

The tour boat *Samuel Slater* on the Blackstone River

## Chepachet

★ **Ancient and Horribles Parade:** If you want a traditional Fourth of July parade with marching bands, don't come to Chepachet. The annual parade here is more about poking fun at people and events than celebrating the nation's birthday. Since 1927, locals have donned strange costumes and made wacky floats, but traditional marching bands and fire trucks take part, too.

## Smithfield

★ **Powder Mill Ledges Wildlife Refuge:** The trails of this wildlife refuge will take you past animals and wildflowers. The site also offers workshops on natural life in Rhode Island.

# WESTERN RHODE ISLAND AND WEST BAY

**THINGS TO DO: Explore the shoreline near Conimicut Point Lighthouse, gaze at the sky at the Seagrave Memorial Observatory, and learn about steam engines and their role in Rhode Island's past.**

Conimicut Point Park

## Warwick

★ **Conimicut Point Park:** This park on Narragansett Bay offers a beach, a playground, fishing, and great views of the water and of Conimicut Point Lighthouse. Built in 1883, the lighthouse was one of the last in the nation to use gas rather than electricity to power its beam.

## Scituate

★ **Seagrave Memorial Observatory:** If you want stars in your eyes, this is the place for you. Frank Seagrave, whose hobby was studying the night sky, built the observatory in 1914. Today, a private group owns the building and its four telescopes, but anyone can come use them on a Saturday night.

### East Greenwich

★ **New England Wireless and Steam Museum:** This little museum covers some big subjects—wireless communications and steam engines. The wireless room features telegraph equipment and some of the first radios. The collection of working steam engines includes one from Rhode Island's Corliss Steam Engine Company, as well as other local manufacturers.

## THE EAST BAY

**THINGS TO DO:** Bike along the shore and enjoy the same view Metacomet once had of his Wampanoag lands.

### Bristol

★ **Coggeshall Farm Museum:** Wonder what life was like on a Rhode Island farm more than 200 years ago? The Coggeshall Farm Museum lets you see for yourself. Actors dressed in 18th-century clothes do the same tasks that farmers did in the 1790s. They press apples into cider and tap maple trees for their sap, which is turned into syrup.

Tapping maple trees at the Coggeshall Farm Museum

★ **Colt State Park:** This park offers a tremendous view of Narragansett Bay. Bike trails wind along the bay and through fruit trees. There's also a dock, a fishing pier, and picnic grounds.

In 1785, Bristol celebrated the Fourth of July with a parade, and it has held one ever since, making it the oldest Independence Day celebration in the country.

★ **Herreshoff Marine Museum:**
Yachting has a long history in
Rhode Island, and the Herreshoff
Manufacturing Company made some
of the world's fastest sailing boats.
Now the company's former plant
is the site of the Herreshoff Marine
Museum, which features Herreshoff
yachts up to 100 years old.

★ **Haffenreffer Museum of
Anthropology:** This museum is
part of Brown University. It was
built on land that served as the
home of Metacomet (King Philip),
the Wampanoag sachem. On the
museum's grounds is a granite
"seat" called King Philip's Throne.
From there, Metacomet could look
out over his people's lands and the
nearby waters. Inside the museum
are collections featuring items from
Native groups across North and
South America, as well as Africa
and Australia.

## Prudence Island

★ **Heritage Foundation of Rhode
Island Park:** Prudence Island, which
is a short ferry ride from Bristol, is
home to only about 150 families.
Most of the island is undeveloped.
The park has great hiking trails that
offer views of birds and the surrounding bay.

# NEWPORT COUNTY

**THINGS TO DO: Explore the
grand mansions of Newport,
help run a lighthouse, and see a green elephant
in Portsmouth.**

## Newport

★ **Naval War College Museum:** This
museum delves into U.S. naval
history, especially events that took
place in Narragansett Bay. No need
to salute!

★ **Cliff Walk:** For the perfect view
of the water and the Newport "cottages" that line it, take a stroll along
the Cliff Walk, a 3.5-mile (5.6 km)
trail that runs between the houses
and the sea. Along the way, you'll
see magnificent mansions such as
the Breakers and Rosecliff.

Mansions along Cliff Walk

★ **God's Little Acre Burial Ground:** This cemetery, which has graves dating to 1718, is the burial site of many of Newport's enslaved Africans and free blacks.

★ **New England Aquarium Exploration Center:** Want to get up close and personal with sea stars or hermit crabs? Then head to the "touch tank" at the Exploration Center, where you can pet some of the sea creatures.

★ **Rose Island Lighthouse:** The lighthouse on Rose Island, which lies more than 1 mile (1.6 km) offshore, was built in 1870. Most visitors explore the island and the lighthouse during the day. The people who rent rooms in the lighthouse and stay the night help run the lights.

Rose Island Lighthouse

### SEE IT HERE!

#### FORT ADAMS

After the War of 1812, Americans wanted more protection from future naval attacks. Fort Adams was constructed in Newport between 1824 and 1857, and it became the largest coastal fort in the United States. The fort was built to hold more than 400 guns, though fewer were actually installed. The fort ceased serving as a military base in the 1950s and is now part of a state park. Each year, two popular music festivals, one for jazz and one for folk, are held just outside Fort Adams's thick stone walls. The grounds around the fort feature ball fields, beaches, and a boat ramp.

★ **Newport Casino:** There's no gambling at this historic casino, which was built in 1880 as a sports club. Today, it's the home of the International Tennis Hall of Fame and a tennis museum. Sports such as tennis and croquet are still played there, too.

## SUPPORTER OF HIS FAITH

Jewish settlers had first reached Rhode Island some 100 years before Aaron Lopez (1731–1782) arrived, but it was Lopez who helped build one of the first synagogues in North America. His family had lived in Portugal before immigrating. They settled in Newport, where they made a fortune producing candles and soap before branching out into shipbuilding and the slave trade. In the early 1760s, Aaron Lopez put up money to build Touro Synagogue. During the American Revolution, Lopez used his business skills to help supply U.S. troops.

★ **Touro Synagogue:** In 1763, the Jewish community in Newport opened one of the first synagogues in the United States. Peter Harrison, a noted colonial architect, designed the building. Today, Touro Synagogue is still used for religious services.

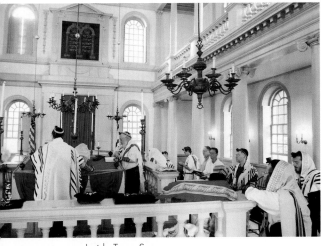

Inside Touro Synagogue

### Tiverton

★ **Butterfly Zoo:** All kinds of butterflies are raised at this farm, which also features a "zoo" filled with the beautiful insects. On sunny days, visitors can stroll through the greenhouse where the butterflies fly, eat, and lay eggs.

### Middletown

★ **Purgatory Chasm:** Above Second Beach is a rocky cliff with a giant chasm, or split, in the rocks. Folk legends say the devil hit the rocks with an ax, resulting in this 160-foot-deep (49 m) chasm. Actually, the movement of glaciers millions of years ago created the split, and more recent sea erosion has added to it. You can cross Purgatory Chasm on a small wooden bridge and see the sea below.

Green Animals Topiary Garden

## Portsmouth

★ **Green Animals Topiary Garden:**
Ever seen a green elephant? You will, at the Green Animals Topiary Garden. A huge elephant and more than 80 other figures have been shaped out of bushes and hedges. The garden, the oldest of its kind in the United States, also has bushy, living sculptures of geometric shapes and fancy designs.

## Jamestown

★ **Beavertail Lighthouse Museum:**
To shed some light on the history of Rhode Island lighthouses, check out this museum. It's housed next to the third-oldest U.S. lighthouse, which was built in 1749. The museum also has an exhibit on the lives of lighthouse keepers.

## SEE IT HERE!

### JAMESTOWN FIRE MUSEUM

Take a trip back in time to see how firefighters in Jamestown battled blazes in the 1800s. The single-story wooden museum building lies in the city's charming historic district. One of the museum's most interesting artifacts is an 1859 hand pump that took 30 to 40 people to operate—and 40 more to pull the wagon by hand! Also on display are old-fashioned breathing equipment, leather water buckets, antique ladders, and hundreds of photographs that show the development of firefighting technology.

## Little Compton

★ **Rhode Island Red Plaque:**
Adamsville, a village within Little Compton, was the birthplace of the first Rhode Island Red chicken, which is now the official state bird. A plaque mounted on a granite stone marks the occasion. The Reds are prized for both their eggs and their meat.

Rhode Island Red chicken

## FAQ

**Q: WHAT IS SOUTH COUNTY?**

**A:** South County isn't really a county at all. It's just a nickname for the towns that form Washington County.

## SOUTH COUNTY

**THINGS TO DO:** Hit the beach at Misquamicut, stroll through the streets of Watch Hill, and enjoy the dancing at a powwow.

### North Kingstown

★ **Quonset Air Museum:** The museum building was once part of the Quonset Point Naval Air Station. Now it traces the role Rhode Island played in U.S. aviation history. On display are military airplanes and helicopters, some dating back to World War II.

### Westerly

★ **Misquamicut State Beach:** Looking for fun in the sun? Join beachgoers from across southern New England at Misquamicut. Along the beach are clam shacks and ice cream shops, an amusement park, and waterslides.

★ **Watch Hill:** This village got its name during the American Revolution, when local residents stood watch for attacking British ships. Today, it boasts quaint shops, a lighthouse, and great beaches.

### New Shoreham

★ **North Light:** Older lighthouses on Block Island were made from wood. The building at North Light is made of granite and iron, so it can withstand almost any storm. The tower is not open to the public, but the lighthouse's first floor has a small museum.

★ **Block Island Southeast Lighthouse National Historic Landmark:** Built in 1875, this five-story lighthouse and attached dwelling is now a museum. Visitors can see the original lighthouse lens with its wicks that were fueled by whale oil.

### Charlestown

★ **Narragansett Indian Powwows:** On their tribal lands and at other sites, Narragansetts hold several powwows each year. People come from far and wide to enjoy the singing, dancing, and food.

Dancer at a Narragansett powwow

# SCIENCE, TECHNOLOGY, ENGINEERING, & MATH PROJECTS

## 120

Make weather maps, graph population statistics, and research endangered species that live in the state.

# PRIMARY VS. SECONDARY SOURCES

## 121

So what are primary and secondary sources? And what's the diff? This section explains all that and where you can find them.

# BIOGRAPHICAL DICTIONARY

## 133

This at-a-glance guide highlights some of the state's most important and influential people. Visit this section and read about their contributions to the state, the country, and the world.

# RESOURCES

Books and much more. Take a look at these additional sources for information about the state.

## 138

# WRITING PROJECTS

## Write a Memoir, Journal, or Editorial for Your School Newspaper!

**Picture Yourself . . .**

★ Building a Narragansett wigwam. You'll need sticks, animal skins, tree bark, and long leaves. Describe how you will put them together.

  **SEE:** Chapter Two, pages 24–25.

★ Taking part in the Dorr Rebellion. Write an editorial for your school newspaper explaining why you believe Rhode Island's voting requirements are unfair and how you want them changed.

  **SEE:** Chapter Four, pages 54–55.

## Create an Election Brochure or Web Site!

Run for office! Throughout this book, you've read about some of the issues that concern Rhode Island today. As a candidate for governor of Rhode Island, create a campaign brochure or Web site.

★ Explain how you meet the qualifications to be governor of Rhode Island.

★ Talk about the three or four major issues you'll focus on if you're elected.

★ Remember, you'll be responsible for Rhode Island's budget. How would you spend the taxpayers' money?

  **SEE:** Chapter Seven, pages 87–89.

## Create an interview script with a famous person from Rhode Island!

★ Research various famous Rhode Islanders, such as Roger Williams, Bill Conti, David Macaulay, Sissieretta Joyner Jones, Ruth Simmons, Seth MacFarlane, Ellison Myers Brown, and many others.

★ Based on your research, pick one person you would most like to interview.

★ Write a script of the interview. What questions would you ask? How would this famous person answer? Create a question-and-answer format. You may want to supplement this writing project with a voice-recording dramatization of the interview.

  **SEE:** Chapter Three, pages 33–39, Chapter Six, pages 78–83, and the Biographical Dictionary, pages 133–137.

# ART PROJECTS

## Create a PowerPoint Presentation or Visitors' Guide

**Welcome to Rhode Island!**

Rhode Island is a great place to visit and to live! From its natural beauty to its bustling cities and historical sites, there's plenty to see and do. In your PowerPoint presentation or brochure, highlight 10 to 15 of Rhode Island's amazing landmarks. Be sure to include:

★ a map of the state showing where these sites are located

★ photos, illustrations, Web links, natural history facts, geographic stats, climate and weather info, and descriptions of plants and wildlife

**SEE:** Chapter Nine, pages 104–115, and Fast Facts, pages 126–127.

## Illustrate the Lyrics to the Rhode Island State Song
**("Rhode Island It's For Me")**

Use markers, paints, photos, collages, colored pencils, or computer graphics to illustrate the lyrics to "Rhode Island It's for Me." Turn your illustrations into a picture book, or scan them into PowerPoint and add music.

**SEE:** The lyrics to "Rhode Island It's for Me" on page 128.

## Research Rhode Island's State Quarter

From 1999 to 2008, the U.S. Mint introduced new quarters commemorating each of the 50 states in the order that they were admitted to the Union. Each state's quarter features a unique design on its reverse, or back.

★ Research the significance of the image. Who designed the quarter? Who chose the final design?

★ Design your own Rhode Island quarter. What images would you choose for the reverse?

★ Make a poster showing the Rhode Island quarter and label each image.

**GO TO:** www.factsfornow.scholastic.com. Enter the keywords **Rhode Island** and look for the link to the Rhode Island quarter.

# SCIENCE, TECHNOLOGY, ART, & MATH PROJECTS

## Graph Population Statistics!

★ Compare population statistics (such as ethnic background, birth, death, and literacy rates) in Rhode Island counties or major cities.

★ In your graph or chart, look at population density and write sentences describing what the population statistics show; graph one set of population statistics and write a paragraph explaining what the graphs reveal.

**SEE:** Chapter Six, pages 72–75.

## Create a Weather Map of Rhode Island!

Use your knowledge of Rhode Island's geography to research and identify conditions that result in specific weather events. What is it about the geography of Rhode Island that makes it vulnerable to things like nor'easters? Create a weather map or poster that shows the weather patterns over the state. Include a caption explaining the technology used to measure weather phenomena and provide data.

**SEE:** Chapter One, pages 13–14.

## Track Endangered Species

Using your knowledge of Rhode Island's wildlife, research which animals and plants are endangered or threatened.

★ Find out what the state is doing to protect these species.

★ Chart known populations of the animals and plants, and report on changes in certain geographic areas

**SEE:** Chapter One, page 17.

Leatherback turtle

# PRIMARY VS. SECONDARY SOURCES

## What's the Diff?

**Your teacher may require at least one or two primary sources and one or two secondary sources for your assignment.** So, what's the difference between the two?

★ **Primary sources are original.** You are reading the actual words of someone's diary, journal, letter, autobiography, or interview. Primary sources can also be photographs, maps, prints, cartoons, news/film footage, posters, first-person newspaper articles, drawings, musical scores, and recordings. By the way, when you conduct a survey, interview someone, shoot a video, or take photographs to include in a project, you are creating primary sources!

★ **Secondary sources are what you find in encyclopedias, textbooks, articles, biographies, and almanacs.** These are written by a person or group of people who tell about something that happened to someone else. Secondary sources also recount what another person said or did. This book is an example of a secondary source.

## Now that you know what primary sources are—where can you find them?

★ **Your school or local library:** Check the library catalog for collections of original writings, government documents, musical scores, and so on. Some of this material may be stored on microfilm.

★ **Historical societies:** These organizations keep historical documents, photographs, and other materials. Staff members can help you find what you are looking for. History museums are also great places to see primary sources firsthand.

★ **The Internet:** There are lots of sites that have primary sources you can download and use in a project or assignment.

# TIMELINE

★ ★ ★

**U.S. Events** | 8000 BCE | **Rhode Island Events**

**c. 8000 BCE**
The first humans come to Rhode Island.

**500 BCE**

**c. 500 BCE**
The earliest known year-round village is established on Block Island.

**1200 CE**

**c. 1200 CE**
Algonquians begin to raise corn.

**1400**

**1492**
Christopher Columbus and his crew sight land in the Caribbean Sea.

**1500**

**1500**
Narragansetts are the dominant people in what is now Rhode Island.

**1524**
Giovanni da Verrazzano becomes the first European known to reach Rhode Island.

**1600**

**1607**
The first permanent English settlement in North America is established at Jamestown.

**1620**
Pilgrims found Plymouth Colony, the second permanent English settlement.

**1636**
Roger Williams settles in Providence.

**1638**
Anne Hutchinson and her followers found Portsmouth.

**1639**
William Coddington founds Newport.

**1643**
Roger Williams receives a charter from Parliament.

**1663**
Rhode Island gets a new charter from King Charles II.

Anne Hutchinson

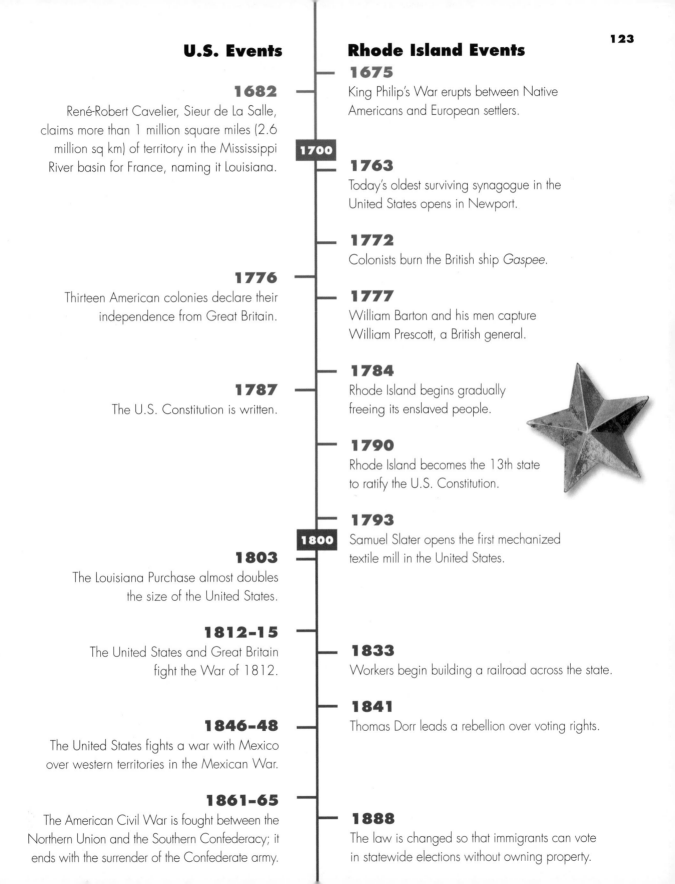

## U.S. Events

**1682**
René-Robert Cavelier, Sieur de La Salle, claims more than 1 million square miles (2.6 million sq km) of territory in the Mississippi River basin for France, naming it Louisiana.

**1776**
Thirteen American colonies declare their independence from Great Britain.

**1787**
The U.S. Constitution is written.

**1803**
The Louisiana Purchase almost doubles the size of the United States.

**1812-15**
The United States and Great Britain fight the War of 1812.

**1846-48**
The United States fights a war with Mexico over western territories in the Mexican War.

**1861-65**
The American Civil War is fought between the Northern Union and the Southern Confederacy; it ends with the surrender of the Confederate army.

## Rhode Island Events

**1675**
King Philip's War erupts between Native Americans and European settlers.

**1700**

**1763**
Today's oldest surviving synagogue in the United States opens in Newport.

**1772**
Colonists burn the British ship *Gaspee*.

**1777**
William Barton and his men capture William Prescott, a British general.

**1784**
Rhode Island begins gradually freeing its enslaved people.

**1790**
Rhode Island becomes the 13th state to ratify the U.S. Constitution.

**1793**
Samuel Slater opens the first mechanized textile mill in the United States.

**1800**

**1833**
Workers begin building a railroad across the state.

**1841**
Thomas Dorr leads a rebellion over voting rights.

**1888**
The law is changed so that immigrants can vote in statewide elections without owning property.

## U.S. Events | 1900 | Rhode Island Events

**1917-18**
The United States engages in World War I.

**1917**
Thousands of Rhode Islanders join the military to fight in World War I.

**1920**
The Nineteenth Amendment to the U.S. Constitution grants women the right to vote.

**1922**
Isabelle Ahearn O'Neill becomes the first female lawmaker in Rhode Island.

**1929**
The stock market crashes, plunging the United States more deeply into the Great Depression.

**1935**
The "Bloodless Revolution" puts the Democratic Party in control of the state government.

**1941-45**
The United States engages in World War II.

**1941-45**
More than 92,000 Rhode Islanders serve in the military during World War II.

**1950-53**
The United States engages in the Korean War.

**1964-73**
The United States engages in the Vietnam War.

**1970**
Save the Bay is formed to limit development near Narragansett Bay.

**1978**
The Narragansett Indians regain their land in Charlestown.

**1980-2000**
Rhode Island's Hispanic population quadruples.

**1991**
The United States and other nations engage in the brief Persian Gulf War against Iraq.

**Early 1990s**
Providence enjoys a "Renaissance."

| 2000 |

**2001**
Terrorists hijack four U.S. aircraft and crash them into the World Trade Center in New York City, the Pentagon in Arlington, Virginia, and a Pennsylvania field, killing thousands.

WaterFire in Providence

**2003**
The United States and coalition forces invade Iraq.

**2010**
Flooding forces thousands of people from their homes.

# GLOSSARY

★ ★ ★

**allies** people who are on the same side in a conflict

**appeals** legal proceedings in which a court is asked to change the decision of a lower court

**archaeologists** people who study the remains of past human societies

**artifacts** items created by humans, usually for a practical purpose

**banished** sent out of a place forever

**charter** a document from a ruler granting rights to a group

**colonies** communities settled in a new land but with ties to another government

**Constitution** the written document that contains all the governing principles of the United States

**corruption** illegal or unfair acts committed by government or business officials

**endangered** in danger of becoming extinct

**federal** relating to the national government

**genetic engineering** changing genes, the chemicals in plants and animals that determine the traits passed from one generation to the next

**glaciers** slow-moving masses of ice

**integrated** brought together all members of society

**Parliament** the legislature in Great Britain

**patriots** Americans who supported independence from Great Britain

**plantation** a large farm that grows mainly one crop

**prejudice** an unreasonable hatred or fear of others

**privateers** private citizens given government approval to capture enemy ships

**reservoir** an artificial lake or tank for storing water

**rogue** a dishonest or worthless person

**smuggle** to bring in or take out illegally

**strike** an organized refusal to work, usually as a sign of protest about working conditions

# FAST FACTS

★ ★ ★

## State Symbols

| | |
|---|---|
| **Statehood date** | May 29, 1790, the 13th state |
| **Official state name** | State of Rhode Island and Providence Plantations |
| **Origin of state name** | Named after the island of Rhodes in the Mediterranean Sea by explorer Giovanni da Verrazzano |
| **State capital** | Providence |
| **State nickname** | Little Rhody, the Ocean State |
| **State motto** | Hope |
| **State bird** | Rhode Island Red chicken |
| **State flower** | Violet |
| **State rock** | Cumberlandite |
| **State mineral** | Bowenite |
| **State shell** | Quahog |
| **State song** | "Rhode Island It's for Me" |
| **State tree** | Red maple |
| **State fair** | Richmond, mid-August |

State seal

## Geography

| | |
|---|---|
| **Total area; rank** | 1,545 square miles (4,002 sq km); 50th |
| **Land; rank** | 1,045 square miles (2,707 sq km); 50th |
| **Water; rank** | 500 square miles (1,295 sq km); 41st |
| **Inland water; rank** | 178 square miles (461 sq km); 46th |
| **Coastal water; rank** | 9 square miles (23 sq km); 20th |
| **Territorial water; rank** | 314 square miles (813 sq km); 17th |
| **Geographic center** | Kent, 1 mile (1.6 km) southwest of Crompton |
| **Latitude** | 41°09' N to 42°01' N |
| **Longitude** | 71°07' W to 71°53' W |
| **Highest point** | Jerimoth Hill, 812 feet (247 m) above sea level |
| **Lowest point** | Sea level along the Atlantic Ocean |
| **Largest city** | Providence |
| **Longest river** | Blackstone |
| **Counties** | 5 |

# Population

| | |
|---|---|
| **Population; rank (2010 census)** | 1,052,567; 43rd |
| **Density (2010 census)** | 1,018 persons per square miles (393 per sq km) |
| **Population distribution (2010 census)** | 91% urban, 9% rural |
| **Ethnic distribution (2010 census)** | White persons: 76.4% |
| | Persons of Hispanic or Latino origin: 12.5% |
| | Black persons: 5.2% |
| | Asian persons: 3.0% |
| | Persons reporting two or more races: 1.9% |
| | Persons of a different race: 0.7% |
| | American Indian and Alaska Native persons: 0.3% |

# Weather

| | |
|---|---|
| **Record high temperature** | 104°F (40°C) at Providence on August 2, 1975 |
| **Record low temperature** | −28°F (−33°C) at Wood River Junction on January 11, 1942 |
| **Average July temperature, Providence** | 74°F (23°C) |
| **Average January temperature, Providence** | 29°F (−2°C) |
| **Average yearly precipitation, Providence** | 47 inches (119 cm) |

State flag

# STATE SONG

★ ★ ★

## "Rhode Island It's for Me"

The state song was written by Charlie Hall, with music by Maria Day. It was adopted in 1996.

I've been to every state we have
but I think that I'm inclined,
To say that Rhody stole my heart;
You can keep the forty-nine.

Herring gulls that dot the sky
Blue waves that paint the rocks
Water rich with Neptune's life
The boats that line the docks.

I see the lighthouse flickering
to help the sailors see.
There is a place for everyone
Rhode Island it's for me!

Chorus:
Rhode Island, oh Rhode Island,
Surrounded by the sea
Some people roam
the earth for home
Rhode Island's it for me.

I love the fresh October days,
The buzz on College Hill.
Art that moves an eye to tear,
A jewelers special skill.

Icicles refract the sun,
Snow falling gracefully.
Some people search
for a place that's warm
Rhode Island's it for me.
(Chorus)

The skyline piercing Providence,
The state house dome so rare.
Residents who speak their minds
No longer unaware.

Roger Williams would be proud to see
His "colony"
So don't sell short this precious port:
Rhode Island's it for me.
(Chorus)

# NATURAL AREAS AND HISTORIC SITES

### National Memorial

Rhode Island's sole national memorial, the *Roger Williams National Memorial*, honors the life of the founder of Rhode Island who championed the ideal of religious freedom.

### National Heritage Corridor

The *John H. Chafee Blackstone River Valley National Heritage Corridor* covers 400,000 acres (162,000 ha) and is unusual in the national park system because the federal government manages no part of it. This heritage corridor features the cities, towns, people, and culture of the valley where the American Industrial Revolution began.

### National Historic Site

Rhode Island's only national historic site is the *Touro Synagogue National Historic Site*. This synagogue is the oldest surviving synagogue in the United States.

### State Parks and Forests

Rhode Island's state park system features 19 state parks and beach areas, including *Beavertail State Park* in Narragansett Bay, *Colt State Park* in Bristol, and *Misquamicut State Beach* in Westerly.

Inside Touro Synagogue

# SPORTS TEAMS

★ ★ ★

## NCAA Teams (Division I)

Brown University *Bears*
Providence College *Friars*
University of Rhode Island *Rams*

The University of Rhode Island Rams in action against
Nebraska's Creighton University

# CULTURAL INSTITUTIONS

★ ★ ★

## Libraries

The *Providence Public Library* has many specialized collections, including the the Rhode Island Collection.

The *Rhode Island State Archives* contains materials on the state's history, including documents dating back to 1638 and thousands of photographs.

*University Library*, at the University of Rhode Island in Kingston, has a special collections department, which contains many rare books and manuscripts along with a collection of interviews on local history.

The *Rhode Island Historical Society Library* in Providence has the state's most significant archive for local history.

## Museums

The *Museum of Natural History* (Providence) has a fantastic collection of insects, birds, and fossils, along with an exhibit on geology. Cormack Planetarium, part of the museum, has a telescope for viewing the moon.

The *Museum of Newport History* (Newport) includes ceramics, drawings, needlework, and paintings pertaining to the history of the area. Musical instruments are also on display.

The *Rhode Island Black Heritage Society Museum* (Providence) has information on the history of African Americans in Rhode Island, including photographs, paintings, documents, manuscripts, and letters.

The *Rhode Island School of Design Museum* (Providence) holds more than 80,000 pieces of art, ranging from impressionist paintings to Chinese sculpture. It also has an Egyptian gallery with an actual coffin and mummy.

## Performing Arts

The *Rhode Island Philharmonic Orchestra* (East Providence) performs classical music series, informal concerts, and holiday shows.

The *Theatre Company of Rhode Island* stages comedies, dramas, musicals, and murder mysteries at the Assembly Theatre in Harrisville.

## Universities and Colleges

In 2011, Rhode Island had 2 public and 10 private institutions of higher learning.

# ANNUAL EVENTS

## January–March

**New Year's Day Plunge Swimming events** in Newport, Wickford, and Jamestown (January)

**Winter Sports Carnival** in Providence (February)

**Rhode Island Spring Flower and Garden Show** in Providence (February)

**Newport Irish Heritage Month** (March)

## April–June

**May Breakfasts** around the state (May)

**Festival of Historic Houses** in Providence (June)

**Gaspee Days Colonial Encampment** in Warwick (June)

**Newport–Bermuda Yacht Race** (biennially in June)

**Providence Festival Chorus Concert** (June)

**Invitational Block Island Sound Horton Race** at Watch Hill (June)

## July–September

**Bristol Fourth of July Parade**

**Black Ships Festival** in Newport (July)

**Hall of Fame Tennis Championships** in Newport (July)

**Newport Music Festival** (July)

**Rhode Island Red Chicken Barbecue** in Little Compton (August)

**Wickford Art Festival** (July)

**Charlestown Chamber Seafood Festival** (August)

**Newport Jazz Festival** in Newport (August)

**Rhode Island Open Saltwater Fishing Derby** (August–November)

**Dragon Boat Races** in Pawtucket (September)

**Providence Waterfront Festival** (September)

## October–December

**Autumnfest** in Woonsocket (October)

**Antique Auto Tour**, Woonsocket to Westerly (October)

**Scituate Art Festival** (October)

**Native American Heritage Day Pow Wow** in Warwick (November)

**Christmas in Newport** (December)

# BIOGRAPHICAL DICTIONARY

Avi

**Avi (1937–)** is a popular writer of children's books. He spent some of his most productive years in Providence.

**Natalie Babbitt (1932–)** is a children's book writer who was born in Ohio and later moved to Providence. Her book *Tuck Everlasting* was made into a film.

**Edward Bannister** See page 80.

**William Barton (1748–1831)** of Warren served as a general during the American Revolution.

**William Blackstone (1595–1675)** was a minister who moved from Massachusetts to what is now Cumberland, becoming the first European to settle in Rhode Island.

**Don Bousquet (1948–)** is a cartoonist known for poking fun at his native state. His work appears in the *Providence Journal* and other publications.

**Ellison Myers Brown** See page 83.

**John Brown (1736–1803)** was a member of the wealthy Brown family of Providence who made a fortune in the slave trade.

**Moses Brown (1738–1836)** was a member of the wealthy Brown family of Providence. After earning some money in the slave trade, he turned against slavery. He helped Samuel Slater open the first mechanized textile mill in the United States. He and his brothers founded Brown University.

**Kady Brownell (c. 1842–1915)** was the wife of a Rhode Island soldier, and she went with him to fight in the Civil War. She was recognized for her bravery on the battlefield.

**Ambrose Burnside (1824–1881)** was a native of Indiana who moved to Bristol, Rhode Island. He served as a general in the Civil War, and his name is the source for the word *sideburns*.

**Canonicus (1565?–1647)** was a Narragansett sachem who sold land to Roger Williams.

Ambrose Burnside

Blu Cantrell

**Blu Cantrell (1976–)** was born Tiffany Cobb in Providence. She is an R & B and soul singer and songwriter.

**Wendy Carlos (1939–)** was a pioneer in electronic music. She recorded a groundbreaking album called *Switched-On Bach* that featured a synthesizer, an unknown instrument at the time. She is a native of Pawtucket.

**Elizabeth Buffum Chace** See page 57.

**William Coddington (1601–1678)** was a supporter of Anne Hutchinson and founded Newport. He later served as governor of the colony.

**George M. Cohan (1878–1942)** was a songwriter and entertainer best known for composing classics such as "Give My Regards to Broadway," "I'm a Yankee Doodle Dandy," and "You're a Grand Old Flag." A native of Providence, he began his career as a young child performing in a vaudeville act with his family.

**Bill Conti (1942–)** is a composer and conductor. The Providence native has written the music for many films, including the *Rocky* movies.

**George Corliss (1817–1888)** was a New York native who started a business in Providence making steam engines. He made improvements to existing engines and built some of the most powerful ones of the day.

**Michael Corrente (1959–)** is a film director from Pawtucket. Several of his films, including *Outside Providence* and *Federal Hill*, have been set in Providence.

**Matt Cottam** See page 102.

**Jill Craybas (1974–)** is a former professional tennis player who was the 1996 NCAA singles champion. She was born in Providence.

**Viola Davis (1965–)** is a stage and screen actor who grew up in Central Falls. She has earned two Tony Awards, for her performances in *King Hedley II* and *Fences*, and has two Academy Award nominations, for *Doubt* and *The Help*.

Jill Craybas

Peter (left) and Bobby Farrelly

**Thomas Dorr (1805–1854)** was a Providence native who fought for greater voting rights for the state's residents and led the Dorr Rebellion, which resulted in Rhode Island's first constitution.

**Peter Farrelly (1956–)** and **Bobby Farrelly (1958–)**, natives of Cumberland, are a film writing and directing team. They have made many successful films, including *Dumb and Dumber*.

**Ann Smith Franklin (1696–1763)** was America's first female newspaper editor and the publisher of Newport's *Mercury* newspaper. Her husband, James, was Benjamin Franklin's brother.

**John Goddard (1724–1785)** of Newport was the leading cabinetmaker of his day. Today his work is extremely valuable.

**Jabez Gorham (1792–1869)** was a Providence silversmith who founded a company in 1842 that produced fine silver items.

**Samuel Gorton (1592–1677)** was a religious leader banished from Massachusetts. He settled in Rhode Island and founded the town of Warwick.

**Robert Gray (1755–1806)** was a native of Tiverton who sailed around the world and explored what became the northwest United States.

**Theodore Francis Green** See page 64.

**Nathanael Greene** See page 46.

**Henry Hassenfeld** See page 101.

**Raymond Hood (1881–1934)** was an architect who designed buildings in the art deco style of the 1920s and 1930s. Among his most famous buildings are Rockefeller Center and the McGraw-Hill Building in New York City and the Tribune Tower in Chicago. He was born in Pawtucket.

**John Christian Hopkins (1960–)** is a member of the Narragansett Nation who writes about Indian affairs for several newspapers and has written a book about the aftermath of King Philip's War.

**Julia Ward Howe** See page 81.

**Alice Winsor Hunt (1872–1968)** was a relative of Roger Williams noted for her social work. She led the fight to protect children in the workplace.

**Anne Hutchinson** See page 35.

**Sissieretta Joyner Jones** See page 82.

Raymond Hood

**Jhumpa Lahiri (1967–)** is a short story writer and novelist whose work often centers on the lives of Indian immigrants and their children. Her first book, *Interpreter of Maladies*, won the Pulitzer Prize for Fiction in 2000. She grew up in Kingston.

**Napoleon "Nap" Lajoie (1874–1959)**, a native of Woonsocket, was a professional baseball player from 1896 to 1916. In 1901, he batted .426—a mark that has never been equaled. He was elected to the Baseball Hall of Fame in 1937.

**Ida Lewis** See page 58.

**Charles I. D. Looff (1852–1918)** was born in Denmark and later moved to Providence. He is remembered for the carousels he created for parks throughout the United States.

**Davey Lopes (1945–)** was a second baseman for the Los Angeles Dodgers for 10 years before becoming a manager and coach in the major leagues. He was born in East Providence.

**H. P. Lovecraft (1890–1937)**, a native of Providence, wrote strange, dark science fiction and horror stories. His work greatly influenced later writers.

Debra Messing

**David Macaulay (1946–)** is a graduate of the Rhode Island School of Design in architecture. He writes books that explain the construction of different kinds of buildings. His works include *Cathedral* and *The Way Things Work*.

**Seth MacFarlane (1973–)** is a graduate of the Rhode Island School of Design and the creator of the TV cartoon *Family Guy*, which is set in Rhode Island.

**Debra Messing (1968–)** is a TV and film actor. She grew up in East Greenwich, outside of Providence.

**Metacomet** See page 39.

**Vinny Paz (Pazienza) (1962–)**, a native of Cranston, is a former world champion boxer in the lightweight and middleweight divisions. He was nicknamed the Pazmanian Devil for his aggressive style of boxing.

**Annie Smith Peck (1850–1935)** was a mountain climber and scholar. In 1908, the Providence native became the first person to climb Mount Huascarán, a towering peak in Peru.

Davey Lopes

**Matthew Perry (1794–1858)** was a U.S. naval commander in the Mexican-American War and the War of 1812. He was instrumental in opening up Japan to Western trade. Born in Newport, he was the younger brother of Oliver Hazard Perry.

**Oliver Hazard Perry (1785–1819)**, a native of South Kingstown, was a naval hero who commanded the U.S. fleet on the Great Lakes during the War of 1812. He led U.S. forces to a victory over the British, giving Americans control of the Great Lakes.

**Jack Reed** See page 19.

**Elizabeth Roberts** See page 89.

**Duke Robillard (1948–)** is a blues guitar player who performed with the popular bands Roomful of Blues and the Fabulous Thunderbirds. Born in Woonsocket, he's won several W. C. Handy Awards for Best Blues Guitarist of the Year.

**Ruth J. Simmons (1945–)** is the former president of Brown University. The great-granddaughter of slaves, she was the first African American to serve as president of an Ivy League school.

**Sherwood Spring (1944–)** was an astronaut who served aboard the space shuttle *Atlantis* in 1985. He grew up in Harmony.

**Gilbert Stuart (1755–1828)** was born in North Kingstown and went to Europe to study painting. He later painted many important figures in early American history, including George Washington.

**Thomas Tew (?–1695)** was known as the Rhode Island Pirate. From his base in Newport, he sailed as far as Africa looking for treasure.

Meredith Vieira

**Giovanni da Verrazzano (1485?–1528)** was an Italian explorer who entered Narragansett Bay in 1524. He was the first European known to visit Rhode Island.

**Meredith Vieira (1953–)** is a television journalist from Providence. After working for a time in her home state, she went on to appear on national TV news shows and serve as a cohost of the *Today* show.

**Jemima Wilkinson (1752–1819)** was the daughter of a Quaker family in Cumberland. She traveled as a preacher, spreading her religious beliefs.

**Roger Williams (c. 1603–1683)** was a Puritan minister who was banished from Massachusetts for his religious views. He founded Providence in 1636 and helped Rhode Island become a colony.

**James Woods (1947–)**, who grew up in Warwick, is a film and television actor. He has starred in the TV series *Shark* and appeared in films such as *Ghosts of Mississippi*.

James Woods

# RESOURCES

★ ★ ★

## BOOKS

### Nonfiction

Cunningham, Kevin. *The Rhode Island Colony*. New York: Children's Press, 2011.

Cunningham, Kevin, and Peter Benoit. *The Wampanoag*. New York: Children's Press, 2011.

Kavanagh, James. *Rhode Island Wildlife: An Introduction to Familiar Species*. Dunedin, Fla.: Waterford Press, 2012.

Reilly-McGreen, M. E. *Revolutionaries, Rebels & Rogues of Rhode Island*. Charleston, S.C.: History Press, 2011.

Reilly-McGreen, M. E. *Rhode Island Legends: Haunted Hallows & Monsters' Lairs*. Charleston, S.C.: History Press, 2012.

Slavicek, Louise Chipley. *Anne Hutchinson*. New York: Chelsea House, 2011.

### Fiction

Avi. *Something Upstairs: A Tale of Ghosts*. New York: Orchard Books, 1988.

Babbitt, Natalie. *Tuck Everlasting*. Santa Barbara, Calif.: ABC-CLIO, 1975.

Curtis, Alice Turner. *A Little Maid of Narragansett Bay*. Bedford, Mass.: Applewood Books, 1915.

Licameli, Doris. *Rowing to the Rescue: The Story of Ida Lewis, Famous Lighthouse Heroine*. Morrisville, N.C.: Lulu Enterprises, 2006.

Lisle, Janet Taylor. *Black Duck*. New York: Sleuth/Philomel, 2006.

**FACTS FOR NOW**

Visit this Scholastic Web site for more information on Rhode Island:
**www.factsfornow.scholastic.com**
Enter the keywords **Rhode Island**

# INDEX

★　★　★

# AUTHOR'S TIPS AND SOURCE NOTES

★  ★  ★

Growing up in Connecticut, I spent a great deal of time in Rhode Island, lounging on beaches, getting lost in Providence, and exploring the streets of Newport. Wherever I went, I was impressed by the history and natural beauty of the smallest state.

To research this book, I visited Rhode Island. I also read many books. Particularly helpful were *Rhode Island: A History* by Brown University historian William G. McLoughlin, and *Rhode Island: A Genial History* by local reporters Paul F. Eno and Glenn Laxton. Details on sites I didn't visit myself came from Web sites and sources such as *Off the Beaten Path: Rhode Island* by Robert Curley. For some of the lesser-known facts about the state, I turned to Ryder Windham's *You Know You're in Rhode Island When . . . .* The State of Rhode Island Web sites and the *Providence Journal* site were essential for information on the state government, economy, and current affairs.

**Photographs ©:** age fotostock: 8, 9 left (Glasshouse Images), 70, 71 left (Jenny Acheson), back cover (Renée Comet); Alamy Images: 73 (David H. Wells), 83 bottom (Mark Box/Southcreek Global/Zumapress. com), 38 (North Wind Picture Archives), cover (Randy Duchaine), 19 (Zuma Press); Alexander Nesbitt: 14; AP Images: 133 bottom, 135 bottom (Bettmann/Corbis), 133 top (Jim Shea), 89 (Joe Giblin), 130 center (Nati Harnik), 96, 97 left (Stephan Savoia), 63 bottom, 93, 103, 107 left, 115, 124 left (Stew Milne), 134 bottom (Tsugufumi Matsumoto), 18 (Victoria Arocho), 83 top, 90; Art Resource, NY: 81 (National Portrait Gallery/Smithsonian Institution), 80 top (Smithsonian American Art Museum, Washington, DC); Aurora Photos/Michael Winokur: 114 right; Bridgeman Art Library International Ltd., London/New York: 79 top (Museum of Fine Arts, Houston, Texas/The Bayou Bend Collection, gift of Miss Ima Hogg), 35 top, 122 (Schlesinger Library, Radcliffe Institute, Harvard University), 51 (Smithsonian Institution, Washington, DC); Brown Brothers: 40; Cat Laine: 80 bottom; Corbis Images: 112 right (Atlantide Phototravel), 52, 65 (Bettmann), 111, 114 left (Bob Krist), 78 top, 106 left (Bob Rowan/Progressive Image), 108 (David H. Wells), 58 bottom (G.E. Kidder Smith), 134 top (Gene Blevins), 63 top right, 67 (Hulton-Deutsch Collection), 59, 62 top, 63 top left (Lewis Wickes Hines), 137 top (Nancy Kaszerman/Zuma), 12 (Nubar Alexanian), 4 bottom right, 97 right, 99 (Onne van der Wal), 134 top (Steve Marcus/Reuters), 5 top left, 49 top right, 56, 60; Dembinsky Photo Assoc./Marilyn Kazmers: 4 top left, 15 bottom; Envision Stock Photography Inc.: 4 bottom left, 71 right, 76, 77 right (Madeline Polss), 77 left (Rebecca Imbimbo); Everett Collection, Inc.: 136 top (Michael Germana), 137 bottom (Monty Brinton/CBS), 61 (Wisconsin Historical Society), 47, 55, 62 bottom, 64; Getty Images: 66 (J.R. Eyerman/Time Life Pictures), 113 left, 129 (John Nordell), 4 top center, 21 top right, 27 (MPI); Courtesy of Hasbro, Inc.: 101; ImageState/The Print Collector/Heritage-Images: 28 bottom; Inmagine: 94, 127; iStockphoto: 130 top (David Freund), 5 bottom right, 113 right (Gene Chutka), 116 bottom, 130 bottom (Geoffrey Black), 20 bottom (Greg Nicholas), 4 top right, 29 bottom, 123 (Hannamaria Photography), 106 right (Nicky Gordon), 128 (Vladislav Lebedinski); Landov: 84, 85 left (Jessica Rinaldi/Reuters), 136 bottom (Bill Greenblatt/UPI Photo); Courtesy of Matt Cottam: 102; Minden Pictures/Frans Lanting: 17 bottom, 120; National Geographic Stock/Todd Gipstein: 22; North Wind Picture Archives: 20 top, 21 top left, 21 bottom, 24, 25, 28 top, 29 top left, 31, 36, 46, 48 top, 49 top left, 54; Photo Researchers, NY/Jim Zipp: 17 top; PhotoEdit/Dennis MacDonald: 85 right, 87; Photolibrary/Sharon Green/Pacific Stock: 132; Richard Benjamin/www.photosofRI.com: 5 bottom left, 79 bottom, 107 right, 109, 110, 112 left; Superstock, Inc./BlueGreen Pictures: cover inset; The Art Archive/Picture Desk: 37; The Granger Collection, New York: 29 top right, 32, 43, 58 top, 82; The Image Works: 5 top right, 69, 124 right (Andre Jenny), 44 (ARPL/HIP), 39 (Mary Evans Picture Library), 9 right, 16 (Peter Hvizdak), 48 bottom (SSPL), 35 bottom (The Image Works Archives); US Mint: 116 top, 119; Vector-Images.com/Uvex: 4 bottom center, 95, 126; Veer/Brand X Photography: 121; Wikipedia: 49 bottom, 57.

Maps by Map Hero, Inc.